BLACK
SPORTS
HEROES

Past and Present

By

MORRIE TURNER

Order this book online at www.trafford.com
or email orders@trafford.com

Most Trafford titles are also available at major online book retailers.

Printed in the United States of America.

ISBN: 978-1-4269-7652-0 (sc)
ISBN: 978-1-4269-7653-7 (hc)
ISBN: 978-1-4269-7654-4 (e)

Library of Congress Control Number: 2011914529

Trafford rev. 10/25/2011

www.trafford.com

North America & international
toll-free: 1 888 232 4444 (USA & Canada)
phone: 250 383 6864 ♦ fax: 812 355 4082

CONGRATULATIONS TO MORRIE TURNER FOR THIS IMPRESSIVE COMPILATION OF BLACK HISTORY ABOUT "GREAT BLACK ATHLETES" THE SKILLFUL WAY HE COMBINES HUMOR WITH FACTS MAKES THE READING NOT ONLY INTERESTING, BUT MORE IMPORTANTLY PROVIDES AN EDUCATIONAL TOOL WHICH MOST SURELY WILL APPEAL TO AND INSPIRE READERS OF ALL AGES.

BEST WISHES, AND CONTINUE YOUR GOOD WORK.
YOURS IN FRIENDSHIP,
AL ATTLES

GOLDEN STATE
WARRIORS

Dedicated to my Favorite Athletes,

MY GREAT-GRANDCHILDREN:

JORDAN, MICHAELA, SHELBY, SHANE, ANTHONY, JASMINE AND soon CAMERON

Acknowledgements

Research: Karol Trachtenberg

Editing: Jeannette Eagan

Lettering: Sid Shaffer

Lettering: Roshaan Rogers

TABLE OF CONTENTS

Baseball

FAMOUS BLACK FIRSTS IN BASEBALL

JACKIE ROBINSON
1919-1972

HE BROKE BASEBALL'S COLOR LINE IN 1947 WITH THE BROOKLYN DODGERS. HE WAS THE FIRST AFRICAN-AMERICAN ENSHRINED IN BASEBALL'S HALL OF FAME.

HE FIRST STARRED IN FOOTBALL, BASKETBALL AND TRACK AT UCLA BEFORE SERVING IN THE ARMY IN WWII, THEN IN THE NEGRO LEAGUES.

AFTER HIS PLAYING DAYS WERE OVER HE CHAMPIONED THE COURSE OF BLACKS IN THE CIVIL RIGHTS ARENA.

BASEBALL SCRAMBLE QUIZ

CAN YOU UNSCRAMBLE THE LAST NAMES OF THE BASEBALL PLAYERS PICTURED BELOW. USE THE FACTS BELOW THE PICTURE TO AID YOU.

1.

CURT
DOLFO

HE WAS RAISED IN OAKLAND, (CA.) AND WAS AN ALL-STAR CENTER-FIELDER FOR THE ST. LOUIS CARDINALS. HE CHALLENGED MAJOR LEAGUE BASEBALL'S RESERVE CLAUSE, WHICH TIED PLAYERS TO ONE TEAM FOR THE LENGTH OF THEIR CAREERS UNLESS THE TEAM ELECTED TO TRADE THEM.

THOUGH HIS CASE FAILED IN THE COURTS, IT ULTIMATELY HELPED BRING ON FREE AGENCY.

NAME: _____

DAN BANKHEAD (1920-76) A MEMBER OF BROOKLYN DODGERS, WAS THE FIRST BLACK PITCHER IN THE MAJOR LEAGUES AUG. 26, 1947.

2.

JOE
GOMRAN

HE PLAYED ON CONSECUTIVE WORLD CHAMPION CINCINNATI REDS TEAMS IN 1975 AND '76, WON THE NAT'L. LEAGUES MOST VALUABLE PLAYER AWARD TWICE, RECEIVED SEVERAL GOLD GLOVES FOR FIELDING EXCELLENCE.
ACCOMPLISHMENTS: GAME WINNING HITS IN 1972 ALL STAR GAME AND 3RD & 7TH GAMES OF '75 SERIES WHICH GAVE REDS THE WORLD CHAMPIONSHIP.
NAME: _____

FAMOUS BLACK FIRSTS in BASEBALL

JULY 5 1947

Larry Doby

FIRST BLACK PLAYER IN THE AMERICAN LEAGUE, THE CLEVELAND INDIANS

BASEBALL PROfiles

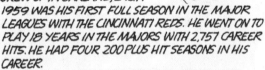

VADA PINSON

BORN IN MEMPHIS, TN., HE GREW UP IN OAKLAND, CALIF.
1959 WAS HIS FIRST FULL SEASON IN THE MAJOR LEAGUES WITH THE CINCINNATI REDS. HE WENT ON TO PLAY 18 YEARS IN THE MAJORS WITH 2,757 CAREER HITS. HE HAD FOUR 200 PLUS HIT SEASONS IN HIS CAREER.
HE HELPED LEAD CINCINNATI TO THE NATIONAL LEAGUE PENNANT IN 1961 WHEN HE HIT .343 WITH 18 HOME RUNS AND 87 RUNS BATTED IN.

BOB GIBSON

A PITCHER WITH ST. LOUIS HE WAS A 20 GAME WINNER 5 TIMES, FIRST PITCHER SINCE WALTER JOHNSON TO RECORD OVER 3,000 LIFETIME STRIKEOUTS. TWICE CY YOUNG AWARD WINNER (1968-70), MVP (1968).

MOSES FLEETWOOD WALKER WAS THE FIRST AFRICAN AMERICAN TO PLAY MAJOR LEAGUE BASEBALL—42 GAMES FOR THE TOLEDO BLUESTOCKINGS IN 1884.

THE BLUESTOCKINGS OF THE AMERICAN ASSOCIATION (MAJOR LEAGUE) DISBANDED AFTER THE '84 SEASON.

©1996 CREATORS SYNP. ALL RIGHTS RESERVED

HE DROVE A BUICK?

4-6

SOUL CIRCLE

1857   1924

MOSES FLEETWOOD WALKER

BASEBALL QUIZ

CAN YOU CHECK THE CORRECT ANSWERS TO THE FACTS LISTED UNDER THE PICTURES OF THESE STAR BASEBALL PLAYERS BELOW.

①

HANK AARON

APRIL 8, 1974 HE HIT HOME-RUN NUMBER 715, BREAKING THE RECORD OF BABE RUTH. HE ENDED HIS CAREER WITH HOW MANY HOME-RUNS.

A.) 720
B.) 755
C.) 738

②

REGGIE JACKSON

A MAJOR LEAGUE HOME-RUN HITTING HALL OF FAME OUTFIELDER. WHICH OF THESE TEAMS DIDN'T HE PLAY FOR.

A) FLORIDA MARLINS
B) NEW YORK YANKEES
C) OAKLAND A'S

WHO AM I?

I WAS BORN IN GEORGIA AND RAISED IN PITTSBURGH. I WAS A LEGENDARY HOME-RUN HITTING CATCHER FOR THE HOMESTEAD GRAYS OF THE NEGRO NATL. LEAGUE.

SATCHEL PAIGE INSISTED THAT I WAS THE TOUGHEST HITTER HE EVER PITCHED TO. I HELPED MY TEAM WIN 9 STRAIGHT PENNANTS BETWEEN 1937 AND 1945.

I EXCEEDED BABE RUTH'S 714 HOME-RUN RECORD.

THE GREAT PITCHER WALTER JOHNSON SAID OF ME, "HE HITS THE BALL A MILE AND THROWS LIKE A RIFLE. TOO BAD THIS _____ IS A COLORED FELLOW." ONLY MY COLOR KEPT ME OUT OF THE MAJOR LEAGUES. 25 YEARS AFTER MY DEATH I WAS VOTED INTO THE BASEBALL HALL OF FAME.

A.) MARTIN DIHIGO
B.) JUDY JOHNSON
C.) JOSH GIBSON

BILL WHITE

HE PLAYED IN THE NATIONAL LEAGUE FOR 13 YEARS, MAINLY AT FIRST BASE FOR THE ST. LOUIS CARDINALS AND WAS THE FIRST AFRICAN-AMERICAN TO BECOME PRESIDENT OF THE LEAGUE. HE PLAYED ON SIX ALL-STAR TEAMS.

FAMOUS BLACK FIRST IN SPORTS

FRANK ROBINSON

A PRODUCT OF McCLYMONDS HIGH SCHOOL, OAKLAND, CALIF. WAS THE FIRST BLACK MANAGER IN THE MAJOR LEAGUES, SIGNING TO MANAGE THE CLEVELAND INDIANS FOR THE 1975 SEASON.

AS A PLAYER FOR CINCINNATI AND BALTIMORE, HE HIT 586 CAREER HOME RUNS. HE WON THE "MOST VALUABLE PLAYER" AWARD IN BOTH THE NATIONAL AND AMERICAN LEAGUES. HE WAS INDUCTED INTO THE BASEBALL HALL OF FAME IN 1982.

BASEBALL

Nickname Quiz

MANY FAMED AFRICAN-AMERICAN BASEBALL PLAYERS ARE KNOWN BY THEIR NICKNAMES. LISTED ON THE LEFT ARE THE NAMES OF NOTED PLAYERS. ON THE RIGHT IS A LIST OF NICKNAMES. CAN YOU MATCH THE CORRECT NICKNAME ON THE RIGHT WITH THE PLAYER ON THE LEFT? ENTER THE RIGHT LETTER IN THE SPACE PROVIDED.

1. REGGIE JACKSON _____   A. POP
2. WILLIE MAYS _____   B. JACKIE
3. LEROY PAIGE _____   C. RUBE
4. WILLIE McCOVEY _____   D. COOL PAPA
5. WALTER LEONARD _____   E. MISTER OCTOBER
6. JAMES BELL _____   F. SATCHEL
7. WILLIAM JOHNSON _____   G. SAY-HEY KID
8. JOHN HENRY LLOYD _____   H. BUCK
9. ANDREW FOSTER _____   I. JUDY
10. JOHN ROOSEVELT   J. STRETCH
    ROBINSON _____

SHARON RICHARDSON JONES BECAME THE FIRST BLACK WOMAN IN MAJOR LEAGUE BASEBALL ADMINISTRATION WHEN SHE WAS NAMED DIRECTOR OF OUTREACH ACTIVITIES FOR THE OAKLAND ATHLETICS IN 1980.

YOU'RE A DISGRACE TO OUR UNIFORM, RALPH

WHAT UNIFORM RALPH?

DON'T GET TECHNICAL

Diamond QUIZ

CAN YOU GUESS THE RIGHT ANSWER TO THE QUESTIONS ABOUT THESE BASEBALL STARS.

CIRCLE THE CORRECT ANSWER

1.)

RICKEY HENDERSON

BASEBALL'S ALL-TIME BASE — STEALING CHAMP. IN 1982 HE STOLE 130 BASES TOPPING FORMER RECORD HOLDER:

A.) MAURY WILLS

B.) LOU BROCK

C.) DARRYL STRAWBERRY

SAM "TOOTHPICK" JONES

① WAS THE FIRST BLACK PITCHER IN THE MAJOR LEAGUES TO PITCH A NO-HITTER FOR THE CHICAGO CUBS AGAINST THE PITTSBURGH PIRATES.
MAY 12, 1955

2.)

DON NEWCOMBE

A FAST-BALL PITCHER WHO COULD DO BOTH. WAS NAMED ROOKIE OF THE YEAR. HE WAS A 20 GAME WINNER THREE TIMES. WON THE "MOST VALUABLE PLAYER" AWARD, 1956 WHEN HE WON 27, LOST 7.

HE PLAYED FOR THE:

A.) NEW YORK YANKEES

B.) PHILADELPHIA PHILLIES

C.) BROOKLYN DODGERS

3.)

ORLANDO CEPEDA

WHILE PLAYING FOR THE S.F. GIANTS, ST. LOUIS CARDINALS, AND BRAVES FROM 1958 TO 1972 BATTING OVER .300 NINE TIMES ENDING WITH A .297 BATTING AVERAGE WITH 397 HOME RUNS.

HE WON WHICH AWARD?

A.) MOST VALUABLE PLAYER

B.) ROOKIE OF YEAR

C.) COMEBACK PLAYER OF YEAR

IN 1951 THE N.Y. GIANTS FIELDED THE FIRST ALL BLACK OUTFIELD IN MAJOR LEAGUE BASEBALL: WILLIE MAYS ——— MONTE IRVIN HANK THOMPSON

memorable baseball
MOMENTS

OCT. 4, 2001

BARRY BONDS

THE SON OF A FORMER BASEBALL ALL-STAR (BOBBY BONDS) AND THE GOD-SON OF A LEGEND (WILLIE MAYS).

HITS HOME RUN NUMBER 71 BREAKING THE SEASON RECORD OF 70 SET BY MARK M°GUIRE OF THE ST. LOUIS CARDINALS.

HE FINISHED THE SEASON WITH A TOTAL OF 73 HOME RUNS A NEW RECORD.

ELSTON HOWARD
1929 - 1980

BECAME THE FIRST AFRICAN-AMERICAN TO PLAY FOR THE N.Y. YANKEE'S. HE LATER BECAME THE YANKEE'S FIRST BLACK COACH, AND THE FIRST BLACK COACH IN THE AMERICAN LEAGUE.

IN THE 1958 WORLD SERIES HE BECAME THE FIRST BLACK TO WIN THE BABE RUTH AWARD.

Baseball

Who Am I?
II

1971 WAS MY FIRST FULL YEAR IN THE MAJOR LEAGUES, PITCHING FOR THE OAKLAND A'S.

THAT YEAR I HAD A 24-8 RECORD AND A 1.82 ERA. I THREW EIGHT STRAIGHT SHUT OUTS THAT SEASON INCLUDING A NO HITTER AGAINST MINNESOTA.

I WON THE CY YOUNG AWARD AND EARNED THE AMERICAN LEAGUES MOST VALUABLE PLAYER HONORS.
I AM:

A.) "BLUE MOON" ODOM

B.) VIDA BLUE

C.) BOB GIBSON

FERGUSON JENKINS (CHICAGO CUBS) WAS THE FIRST BLACK PITCHER TO WIN 20 GAMES IN 6 CONSECUTIVE YEARS.

Who Are They?

CAN YOU GUESS WHO THESE BALL PLAYERS ARE BY THE INFORMATION SUPPLIED UNDER THEIR PICTURE? CIRCLE THE CORRECT ANSWER

① PITTSBURG PIRATES CAREER LEADER IN HOME RUNS, RUNS BATTED IN AND EXTRA BASE HITS — TIED FOR MOST VALUABLE PLAYER IN 1979

A) DAVE PARKER

B) DARRYL STRAWBERRY

C) WILLIE STARGELL

② 1964 PHILLIES ROOKIE OF THE YEAR. IN 1974. HE LED AMERICAN LEAGUE IN HOME RUNS AND RUN BATTED IN AND WAS VOTED AMERICAN LEAGUE MOST VALUABLE PLAYER

A) RICHIE ALLEN

B) WILLIE STARGEL

C) REGGIE JACKSON

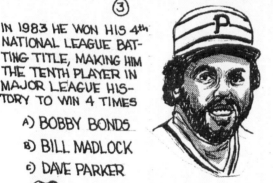

③ IN 1983 HE WON HIS 4th NATIONAL LEAGUE BATTING TITLE, MAKING HIM THE TENTH PLAYER IN MAJOR LEAGUE HISTORY TO WIN 4 TIMES

A) BOBBY BONDS

B) BILL MADLOCK

C) DAVE PARKER

④ HE COLLECTED OVER 3000 CAREER BASE HITS, HAD A CAREER TOTAL 938 STEALS. HE HAD A 19 YEAR SEASON TOTAL, 16½ WITH THE ST. LOUIS CARDINALS

A) LOU BROCK

B) DAVE PARKER

C) RICHIE ALLEN

⑤ HE WAS THE 1983 NATIONAL LEAGUE ROOKIE OF THE YEAR

A) BILL MADLOCK

B) WILLIE STARGELL

C) DARRYL STRAWBERRY

BLACK ACES QUIZ

A PITCHER WHO WINS 20 OR MORE
GAMES IN A SEASON QUALIFIES AS AN
ACE.
BELOW LEFT ARE PITCHERS WHO QUALIFY.
ON THE RIGHT ARE TEAMS THEY WERE WITH
AT THE TIME.
CAN YOU MATCH THE PITCHER WITH HIS TEAM

1. DON NEWCOMBE _____   A. CUBS
2. SAM SAD JONES _____   B. DODGERS
3. JIM "MUDCAT" GRANT __   C. ASTROS
4. BOB GIBSON _____   D. A'S
5. EARL WILSON _____   E. METS
6. FERGUSON JENKINS ____   F. GIANTS
7. AL DOWNING _____   G. MARLINS
8. VIDA BLUE _____   H. TWINS
9. J.R. RICHARD _____   I. TIGERS
10. MIKE NORRIS _____   J. CARDINALS
11. DWIGHT GOODEN _____
12. DAVE STEWART _____
13. DONTRELLE WILLIS ____
14. JUAN MARICHAL _____

DONTRELLE
WILLIS

STRIKE ONE!

STRIKE TWO!

STRIKE THREE!

I GUESS THERE WON'T BE MANY BIDS FOR MY TRADING CARD ON e-BAY!

DIAMOND Notes

LEN COLEMAN

HE BECAME THE SECOND BLACK NATIONAL BASEBALL LEAGUE PRESIDENT WHEN HE REPLACED BILL WHITE, THE FIRST

KEN WILLIAMS

CHICAGO WHITE SOX GENERAL MANAGER. HIS TEAM WON THE 2005 WORD SERIES, THE FIRST IN 88 YEARS

DAN BANKHEAD

WAS THE FIRST BLACK PITCHER IN PITCH IN THE MAJOR LEAGUES (FOR BROOKLYN DODGERS-1947)

WILLIE MAYS

HE STOLE MORE BASES THAN ANY OTHER HOME-RUN HITTER, AND HIT MORE HOME RUNS THAN ANY OTHER BASE STEALER

IN 1951 THE N.Y. GIANTS FIELDED THE FIRST ALL-BLACK OUTFIELD IN THE MAJOR LEAGUES CONSISTING OF WILLIE MAYS, MONTE IRVIN AND HANK THOMPSON

Profile

ROY CAMPANELLA

BROOKLYN DODGERS SUPERB CATCHER AND JACKIE ROBINSON'S TEAMMATE. HE HIT FOR BOTH POWER AND AVERAGE, EXPERT ON DEFENSE AND HANDLING PITCHERS, FROM 1948 TO 1959. A THREE TIME MVP WINNER. AN AUTOMOBILE ACCIDENT ENDED HIS PLAYING CAREER

ERNIE BANKS

HE PLAYED SHORTSTOP FOR CHICAGO CUBS. WON MVP AWARD 1958 AND 1959. HIT 512 HOME RUNS. HE HIT 40 HOME RUNS PER SEASON FIVE TIMES. HE HIT A RECORD FIVE GRAND SLAMS IN 1955 (HE PLAYED NEGRO LEAGUE BALL FOR THE KANSAS CITY MONARCHS)

HORSEHIDE HEROES

EMMETT ASHFORD

THE FIRST BLACK UMPIRE IN MAJOR LEAGUE BASEBALL (FROM 1966 TO 1970) HE UMPIRED IN THE PACIFIC COAST LEAGUE, 1966 TO 70. HE WORKED THE 1967 ALL-STAR GAME AND 1970 WORLD SERIES.

WILLIE McCOVEY

M.V.P. WINNER IN 1969 WHILE WITH THE S.F. GIANTS. 1977 COMEBACK PLAYER OF THE YEAR IN HIS 20TH MAJOR LEAGUE SEASON.
HE HELD THE NATIONAL LEAGUE GRAND SLAM HOME RUN RECORD AT 18.

J.R. (JAMES RODNEY) RICHARD

OF THE HOUSTON ASTROS ESTABLISHED A RECORD FOR STRIKE OUTS BY A RIGHT HANDED PITCHER, 303 IN 1978 AND 313 IN 1979. HE WAS STRICKEN WITH AN EMBOLISM THAT CUT SHORT HIS CAREER.

MAURY WILLS WAS 6 TIME NATIONAL LEAGUE STOLEN BASE LEADER (1960-65) AND BECAME BASEBALL'S THIRD BLACK MANAGER (SEATTLE MARINERS).

I WISH I WAS WHITE

HUH?

BILL WHITE IS A FORMER MAJOR LEAGUE ALL-STAR FIRST BASEMAN...

AND NOW HE'S PRESIDENT OF THE NATIONAL LEAGUE, THE FIRST BLACK TO HEAD A MAJOR LEAGUE SPORTS ORGANIZATION

5-25

BEING BILL WHITE CAN GET YOU INTO BASEBALL GAMES FREE!

SOUL CIRCLE

BILL WHITE

STOPPER QUIZ

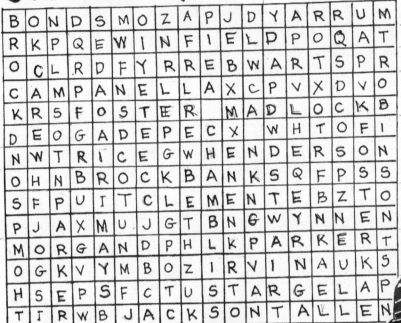

B	O	N	D	S	M	O	Z	A	P	J	D	Y	A	R	R	U	M
R	K	P	Q	E	W	I	N	F	I	E	L	D	P	O	Q	A	T
O	C	L	R	D	F	Y	R	R	E	B	W	A	R	T	S	P	R
C	A	M	P	A	N	E	L	L	A	X	C	P	V	X	D	V	O
K	R	S	F	O	S	T	E	R		M	A	D	L	O	C	K	B
D	E	O	G	A	D	E	P	E	C	X		W	H	T	O	F	I
N	W	T	R	I	C	E	G	W	H	E	N	D	E	R	S	O	N
O	H	N	B	R	O	C	K	B	A	N	K	S	Q	F	P	S	S
S	F	P	U	I	T	C	L	E	M	E	N	T	E	B	Z	T	O
P	J	A	X	M	U	J	G	T	B	N	G	W	Y	N	N	E	N
M	O	R	G	A	N	D	P	H	L	K	P	A	R	K	E	R	T
O	G	K	V	Y	M	B	O	Z	I	R	V	I	N	A	U	K	S
H	S	E	P	S	F	C	T	U	S	T	A	R	G	E	L	A	P
T	I	R	W	B	J	A	C	K	S	O	N	T	A	L	L	E	N

TONY GWYNN

MONTE IRVIN

JIM RICE

DAVE PARKER

GEORGE FOSTER

(16)

MY DAD TOOK ME TO A S.F. GIANTS GAME.

ARE YOU A GIANTS FAN, DIZ?

NAW! I ROOT FOR THAT TEAM WITH ALL THE *BROTHERS*

THE TEAM WITH ALL THE *BROTHERS*?

YEAH, THE HOUSTON AFROS

7-13

MORRIE

HARDBALL QUIZ

CAN YOU ANSWER THESE BASEBALL QUESTIONS? CIRCLE THE RIGHT ANSWER.

① WILLIE MAYS

HE WAS ROOKIE OF THE YEAR IN 1951, WON THE "MOST VALUABLE PLAYER" AWARD IN 1954 AND '65. HE BATTED IN 100 RUNS EACH SEASON BETWEEN 196-67. HIS ELECTRIFYING SPEED DISTINGUISHED HIM FROM OTHER SLUGGERS. HE CAPTURED HOME RUN BATTING TITLES AND GOLD GLOVES. HE RETIRED WHILE WITH THE:

A) S.F. GIANTS   B) N.Y. METS   C) ST. LOUIS CARDINALS

② ROBERTO CLEMENTE

IN THE 1971 WORLD'S SERIES AGAINST THE BALTIMORE ORIOLES HE HAD THE GREATEST SINGLE PERFORMANCE BY ANY PLAYER IN THE FALL CLASSIC, BATTING A 414 AVERAGE, 7 SINGLES, 2 DOUBLES, 1 TRIPLE AND 2 HOME RUNS IN ADDITION TO MAKING 2 IMPOSSIBLE CATCHES IN THE OUTFIELD PLAYING FOR:

A) PHILADELPHIA PHILLIES
B) PITSBURGH PIRATES
C) CHICAGO CUBS

HE DIED IN 1972 IN AN AIRPLANE CRASH WHILE FLYING RELIF SUPPLIES FROM PUERTO RICO TO EARTHQUAKE VICTIMS IN NICARAGUA

How About That?

Derek Jeter, Long time short stop leader and captain of the New York Yankees. He was 1996 Rookie of the Year. He won MVP award for ALL-STAR GAME and World Series in the same year.

Ryan Howard Philadelphia's slugging first baseman, he was 2005 National Rookie of the Year and 2006 MVP and 2006 Nat. League MVP.

C.C. Sabathia Born in Vallejo, CA-his contract signed with the New York Yankees was the most expensive contract for a pitcher in the history of baseball. He was the 2007 CY Young Award Winner

Derrek Lee Born in Sacramento, CA. He was 2005 National League Batting Champion. Gold Glove winner 2003, '05 and '07

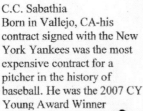

Jimmy Rollins Phillies shortstop born in Oakland, CA. He has stolen at least 20 bases every season since 2001, emulating his childhood baseball hero, Rickey Henderson.

Prince Fielder and his father Cecil Fielder are the only father and son combination to hit 50 home runs in a single season

HOW DID YOU GET SO DIRTY, WELLINGTON?

PRACTICING SLIDING THE BASES LIKE RICKEY HENDERSON DOES, SYBIL

WHO'S HE?

HE'S STOLEN MORE BASES THAN ANY-ONE ELSE IN THE MAJOR LEAGUES

I PITY HIS POOR MOTHER

6-12

PASSPORT QUIZ

Athletes come from all over the world to fill out baseball rosters to make it a truly international game.

Can you guess what country the player listed came from? Possible locations listed below.

Enter Letter of correct location behind name of athlete

1. Pablo Sandoval   Giants ____
2. David Ortiz, Boston Red Sox ____
3. Edgar Renteria, S.F. Giants ____
4. Miguel Tejada, S.F. Giants ____
5. Juan Uribe, L.A. Dodgers ____
6. Albert Pujols, St Louis ____
7. Manny Ramirez ____
8. Pedro Martinez ____

Juan Uribe
L.A. Dodgers

Pablo Sandoval
S.F. Giants

David Ortiz
Boston Red Sox

Miguel Tejada
MVP- American
League-2002

Edgar Renteria
S.F. Giants

Locations	
A) Venezuela	D) Mexico
B) Dominican Republic	E) Santa Domingo
C) Columbia	F) Haiti

NEGRO LEAGUE Baseball #4

JACKIE ROBINSON WAS A TRACK, FOOTBALL AND BASEBALL STAR AT UCLA BEFORE BECOMING A LIEUTENANT IN THE ARMY DURING WORLD WAR II.

AFTER THE WAR, HE PLAYED IN THE NEGRO LEAGUES BEFORE JOINING THE BROOKLYN DODGERS.

WHY WAS HE SENT DOWN?

NEGRO LEAGUE QUIZ

CAN YOU SELECT THE RIGHT ANSWER
TO THE QUESTIONS BELOW?
CIRCLE THE RIGHT ANSWER

WHO AM I?

1.

JAMES "COOL PAPA" BELL

HE SPENT 21 YEARS IN THE NEGRO LEAGUES, THE MEXICAN LEAGUE AND SANTA DOMINGO.
HE HIT FOR HIGH AVERAGES AND WAS A GREAT BASE STEALER KNOWN AS THE FASTEST MAN TO PLAY BASEBALL, WHITE OR BLACK.

HIS POSITION:
A.) SHORTSTOP

B.) OUTFIELDER

C.) CATCHER

2.

BUCK LEONARD

HE BATTED .392 IN 1941 AND LED THE NEGRO LEAGUE, WHILE HITTING 42 HOMERUNS. HE PLAYED 17 YEARS FOR:

A.) BRKLYN. ROYAL GIANTS

B.) HOMESTEAD GRAYS

C.) BALTIMORE STARS

THE FIRST WORLD SERIES BETWEEN NEGRO LEAGUE CLUBS WAS HELD IN 1924.

I WAS A STAR PITCHER IN THE NEGRO LEAGUE LONG BEFORE SIGNING WITH THE CLEVELAND INDIANS IN THE MAJOR LEAGUES. MY FIRST NEGRO LEAGUE TEAM WAS THE BLACK BARONS. THEN THE PITTSBURGH CRAWFORDS WHERE MY FAME GREW. I PITCHED IN SOUTH AMERICA. I BECAME THE FIRST BLACK TO PITCH IN THE AMERICAN LEAGUE.

A.) DON NEWCOMBE
B.) DAN BANKHEAD
C.) LEROY "SATCHEL" PAIGE

NEGRO LEAGUES

ANDREW "RUBE" FOSTER WAS A PITCHER IN "NEGRO BASEBALL"

THEN, AS A MANAGER HE SIGNALED...

HIS PLAYERS WITH PUFFS OF SMOKE FROM A CORNCOB PIPE

HE ESTABLISHED THE FIRST "NEGRO PROFESSIONAL LEAGUE"

BUT COULD HE HIT A CURVE BALL?

ANDREW "RUBE" FOSTER 1879-1930

NEGRO LEAGUE QUIZ II

CAN YOU ANSWER QUESTIONS ABOUT THE STARS OF THE OLD NEGRO LEAGUES. CIRCLE THE CORRECT ANSWERS

1)

MARTIN DIHIGO

HE SPLIT HIS 22 YEARS PLAYING CAREER PLAYING IN THE CUBAN AND NEGRO LEAGUES. RENOWNED FOR HIS VERSATILITY, HE PLAYED EVERY POSITION EXCEPT:

A.) PITCHER

B.) CATCHER

C.) FIRST BASE

HE WAS INDUCTED INTO THE NATIONAL BASEBALL HALL OF FAME IN 1971.

2)

RAY DANDRIDGE

HE HAD A LIFETIME BATTING AVERAGE OF .325 IN A NEGRO AND MEXICO LEAGUES SPANNING 1933 TO 1944. HE WENT FOUR FOR NINE AGAINST MAJOR LEAGUE PITCHER

A.) BOB FELLER

B.) CARL HUBBELL

C.) SAL MAGLIE IN 2 BLACK VS WHITE BASEBALL GAMES

3)

"JUDY" JOHNSON

A SLICK FIELDING THIRD BASEMAN WHO WAS ELECTED INTO NATIONAL BASEBALL HALL OF FAME IN 1975.

HE PLAYED FOR THE:

A.) PITTSBURGH CRAWFORDS

B.) KANSAS CITY MONARCHS

C.) HOMESTEAD GRAYS

Basketball

FAMOUS BLACK FIRSTS in BASKETBALL

BILL RUSSELL

WAS THE FIRST BLACK COACH OF A NATIONAL BASKETBALL ASSOCIATION TEAM (THE BOSTON CELTICS). AN OAKLAND (CA.) McCLYMOND HIGH SCHOOL GRAD, ALL-AMERICAN UNIVERSITY OF SAN FRANCISCO CENTER, '56 OLYMPIC GOLD MEDALIST. HE REVOLUTIONIZED BASKETBALL TACTICS WITH HIS DEFENSE ABILITIES. BILL RUSSELL WAS VOTED MOST VALUABLE LEAGUE PLAYER.

BASKETBALL QUIZ

CAN YOU SELECT THE CORRECT ANSWERS LISTED UNDER THE PICTURES OF THE NOTED BASKETBALL PLAYERS BELOW. (CHECK THE RIGHT ANSWER)

1.)

ISIAH THOMAS

HE HELPED HIS TEAM WIN THE N.C.A.A. CHAMPIONSHIP. HE WAS THE FIRST ROOKIE VOTED AS A STARTER FOR AN NBA ALL-STAR GAME.

HIS PRO TEAM WAS:

A.) DETROIT PISTONS
B.) INDIANA PACERS
C.) NEW YORK KNICKS

2.)

EARVIN "MAGIC" JOHNSON

ACQUIRED BY THE LOS ANGELES LAKERS IN THE 1979-80 SEASON. DESCRIBED AS THE MOST UNMATCHABLE TALENT IN THE NBA. HE LED THE THE LAKERS TO DIVISION AND NBA TITLES AND PLAYED ON THE U.S. OLYMPIC "DREAM TEAM."

WHAT COLLEGE DID HE PLAY FOR?
A.) IOWA STATE
B.) MICHIGAN STATE
C.) MICHIGAN

JOHNNY McLENDON COACHED THE PREDOMINANTLY WHITE PROFESSIONAL TEAM, THE CLEVELAN PIPERS IN THE 1961-62 SEASON BECOMING THE FIRST AFRICAN-AMERICAN TO COACH IN THE AMERICAN BASKETBALL LEAGUE.

(23)

famous BLACK firsts in BASKETBALL

DON BARKSDALE

A BERKELEY (CA.) HIGH SCH-OOL AND U.C.L.A. GRAD WAS THE FIRST AFRICAN-AMERIC-AN TO PLAY ON A U.S. OLYMP-ICS BASKETBALL TEAM (1947 LONDON). HE WAS TEAM CAPT.

HE WAS THE FIRST BLACK SELECTED FOR ALL-AMERICAN HONORS, AND FIRST ELECTED TO THE HELMS ALL-AMATEUR BASKETBALL HALL OF FAME.

ONE OF THE FIRST TO PLAY IN THE N.B.A.

JOHN THOMPSON GEORGETOWN UNV. WAS THE FIRST BLACK COACH TO WIN THE NCAA DIVISI-ON CHAMPIONSHIP —— APRIL 3, 1984

Basketball SCRAMBLE Quiz?

CAN YOU UNSCRAMBLE THE LAST NAMES OF THESE NOTED BASKETBALL PLAYERS. USE THE CLUES UNDER THEIR PICTURES TO AID YOU.

1.

ELGIN LABORY

LOS ANGELES LAKERS COURT WIZARD, THE FIRST OF THE GYMNASTIC STARS, HE REWROTE BASKETBALL HIS-TORY, ONCE SCORING 71 POINTS AGAINST THE NEW YORK KNICKS, THE HIGHEST POINT TOTAL IN A SINGLE GAME AT THE TIME SMASHING HIS OWN NBA RECORD OF 64 POINTS. _____

2.

OSCAR SOINOBRN

A PHENOMENAL PLAYER AT CINCINNATI UNIVERSITY, WINN-ING TRIPLE ALL-AMERICAN HONORS AND SEVEN "PLAYER OF THE YEAR" PRESS AWARDS. HE WAS A MEMBER OF THE GOLD MEDAL WINNING USA OLYMPIC TEAM IN ROME.

HE STARRED WITH AND WAS MVP OF THE CINCINNATI ROYALS. _____

3.

JULIUS RIGVEN

KNOWN AS "DOCTOR J" HE BEC-AME A SUPER STAR. VOTED "MOST VALUABLE PLAYER" TW-ICE IN A ROW. DR. J GAINED HIS FAME WITH THE PHILADELPHIA 76ers.

R⊕UND BALL *Quiz*

CAN YOU GIVE THE CORRECT ANSWERS TO THE QUESTIONS BELOW THESE BASKETBALL PLAYERS? CIRCLE THE RIGHT ANSWER.

1.

MICHAEL JORDAN

HE BECAME THE MOST HERALDED PLAYER IN THE HISTORY OF THE N.B.A. LEADING WHICH TEAM TO SIX WORLD TITLES.

A.) CHICAGO BULLS
B.) MILWAUKEE BUCKS
C.) LOS ANGELES LAKERS

2.

KAREEM ABDUL JABBAR

HE LED U.C.L.A. TO 3 CONSECUTIVE NCAA CHAMPIONSHIPS. HE BECAME THE MOST PROLIFIC SCORER IN NBA HISTORY PLAYING FOR THE LOS ANGELES LAKERS. HIS BIRTH NAME WAS:
A. LEW ALCINDOR
B. MOSES MALONE
C. CHARLES COOPER

HISTORIC MOMENTS IN *Basketball*

MARCH 2, 1962
WILT CHAMBERLAIN
PLAYING FOR THE PHILADELPHIA 76ers SCORED 100 POINTS IN A SINGLE GAME AGAINST THE NEW YORK KNICKS AT HERSHEY, PA. WON BY PHILADELPHIA.

THE FIRST BLACK MANAGER IN ANY SPORT WAS WAYNE EMBRY OF THE MILWAUKEE BUCKS OF THE NBA.

AL ATTLES, A NEWARK, N.J. NATIVE HAS BEEN WITH THE GOLDEN STATE WARRIORS ALL OF HIS CAREER, AS A PLAYER, COACH, VICE-PRESIDENT AND GENERAL MANAGER.

HIS 1974-75 WARRIORS COACHED TEAM IS THE ONLY ONE TO BRING HOME A CHAMPIONSHIP. HIS UNIFORM NUMBER 16 WAS JUST ONE OF 4 EVER RETIRED.

I GUESS IT WAS TOO SWEATY TO WASH.

SOUL CIRCLE

Al Attles

HARDWOOD QUIZ

1.)

KOBE BRYANT

BEFORE SIGNING TO PLAY FOR THE LOS ANGELES LAKERS OF THE N.B.A. HE PLAYED BASKETBALL FOR:

A. U.S. ARMY

B. PHILADELPHI HIGH SCHOOL

C. U.S. NAVY

2.)

EARL MONROE

HE PLAYED ON THE NEW YORK KNICKS WITH WALT FRAZIER WHO WAS KNOWN AS "CLYDE." HIS NICK NAME WAS:

A. THE OYSTER

B. THE SNAKE

C. THE PEARL

3.)

SHAQUILLE O'NEAL

AT 7 FOOT 1 INCH AND 340 LBS. HE IS THE MOST DOMINATING CENTER IN THE NBA. HE PLAYED COLLEGE BALL AT:

A. LSU

B. UCLA

C. FSU

OSCAR ROBINSON WAS THE FIRST BLACK BASKETBALL PLAYER AT THE UNIVERSITY OF CINCINNATTI-HE ALSO PLAYED ON THE 1960 U.S. OLYMPIC GOLD MEDAL TEAM

HE WAS DRAFTED BY THE CINCINNATI ROYALS, THEN TRADED TO THE MILWAUKEE BUCKS, WHERE HE HELPED WIN THE NBA TITLE-HE WAS LATER ELECTED TO THE HALL OF FAME

JUST CALL ME "BIG O"

SURE, OLIVER

SOUL CIRCLE

OSCAR ROBINSON

(26)

CAN YOU UNSCRAMBLE THE NAMES OF
THESE BASKETBALL PLAYERS USING THE
CLUES UNDER THEIR PICTURES TO AID YOU.

1.)

MOSES
NEAMLO
AT THE END OF THE 1982-83
SEASON HE HAD WON THE
NBA "MOST VALUABLE PLAYER"
AWARD FOR 3 OF THE PREV-
IOUS 4 SEASONS.

2.)

WES
LDNSUE
OF THE WASHINGTON BULL-
ETS, WAS THE SECOND PLAY-
ER IN NBA HISTORY TO WIN
THE MVP AND "ROOKIE OF
THE YEAR" THE SAME SEA-
SON.

3.)

WALT
EAFRIRZ
HE WAS FLOOR LEADER AND
PLAY MAKER FOR THE NEW
YORK KNICKS.

4.)

RALPH
NAPOSMS
ONE OF THE GREATEST COLLEGE
BASKETBALL STARS OF ALL
TIME. SIGNED BY THE HOUSTON
ROCKETS. NAMED ROOKIE
OF THE YEAR FOR THE 1983-
1984 SEASON.

5.)

GEORGE
RENIVG
KNOWN AS THE ICEMAN AND CO-
NSIDERED THE BEST PURE SHOOT-
ER IN THE NBA.

6)

CARMELO
HNYAONT

Attended Syracuse Led them to their first national championship in 2003. Named MVP on NCAA EAST Regional, drafted by Denver Nuggets.

7)

STEPHEN
RYCUR

Son of former NBA player. Played for Davidson college. Led Nation in scoring drafted by golden state warriors.

8)

DWIGHT
AWOHDR

He went from So. West Atlanta Christian Academy to center for Orlando Magic, being selected overall in the draft. NBA Defensive Player of the Year 2009-10.

9)

O.J. YOMA

Played college ball at USC, drafted by Minnesota and traded to Memphis.

10)

PAUL
REPEIC

Born in Oakland, CA attended Inglewood high school (Cal) played college ball at Kansas, drafted by Boston Celtics.

11)

TYREKE
SAVEN

Number one pick by Sacramento Kings named "Rookie of the Year" 2009

DUNK QUIZ

CAN YOU COMPLETE THE LAST NAME OF THE BASKETBALL STARS BELOW
USE THE CLUES TO AID YOU

1.)

WILLIS

| R | | | | |

SWING MAN FOR THE WINNING NEW YORK KNICKS OF THE 1960'S FORMER GRAMBLING SCORING ACE. HE WAS THE CORE OF THE KNICKS DEFENSE AND THE MAIN REASON FOR THE KNICKS SUCCESS.

2.)

REGGIE

| | | L | | |

A 3-POINT SHOOTING ACE OF THE INDIANA PACERS, FORMER USC COLLEGE STAR AND MEMBER OF THE "OLYMPIC "DREAM TEAM."

3.)

ALLEN

| | E | | |

HE WAS THE FIRST GUARD SELECTED NO.1 IN THE NBA DRAFT SINCE MAGIC JOHNSON BECAME FLOOR LEADER AND TOP SHOOTER FOR THE PHILADELPHIA 76ers.

4.)

CHARLES

| | | K | | |

HE SCORED 56 POINTS INCLUDING A PLAYOFF RECORD 38 IN THE FIRST HALF FOR PHOENIX SUNS. INDUCTED INTO HALL OF FAME. HE BECAME A BROADCASTER.

5.)

TIM

| | | | C | | |

HE LEAD THE SAN ANTONIO SPURS TO MULTI NBA CHAMPIONSHIPS. A THREE TIME ACC PLAYER OF THE YEAR WITH WAKE FOREST. WAS BEST SHOT BLOCKER IN NCAA HISTORY.

6.)

DOMINIQUE

| | | L | | | |

KNOWN AS THE "HUMAN HIGHLIGHT FILM". HE WON THE 1986 SCORING TITLE AVERAGING 30.3 PER GAME. HE BECAME THE ATLANTA HAWKS ALL TIME POINT LEADER. HE SCORED 51 POINTS IN '86 AGAINST CHICAGO.

CHUCK COOPER BROKE THE NBA'S COLOR BARRIER IN APRIL 1950 WHEN THE BOSTON CELTICS FOUNDER WALTER BROWN SIGNED HIM TO A CONTRACT.

TWO OTHER BLACK PLAYERS WERE SIGNED THAT 1950-51 BASKETBALL SEASON - EARL LOYD AND NAT "SWEETWATER" CLIFTON. LOYD HAD THE DISTINCTION OF BEING THE FIRST BLACK TO PLAY IN AN NBA GAME - 24 HOURS AHEAD OF COOPER.

WHO WAS THE FIRST BLACK WATER BOY?

SOUL CIRCLE

Chuck Cooper

BASKETBALL NICKNAME QUIZ

MANY NOTED BASKETBALL PLAYERS HAVE BEEN KNOWN BY THEIR NICKNAMES. CAN YOU MATCH THE PLAYERS NAMES ON THE LEFT WITH THEIR NICKNAME ON THE RIGHT?

PLACE THE CORRECT LETTER IN THE SPACE PROVIDED.

1. REECE TATUM _____
2. FRED SNOWDEN _____
3. NATHANIEL CLIFTON _____
4. CHARLES COOPER _____
5. WILT CHAMBERLAIN _____
6. JULIUS ERVING _____
7. CLARENCE GAINES _____
8. BOBBY HALL _____

A. DOCTOR "J"
B. SHOWBOAT
C. BIG HOUSE
D. GOOSE
E. THE FOX
F. SWEETWATER
G. THE STILT
H. CHUCK

EARL LLOYD

A STAR AT WEST VIRGINIA STATE BECAME THE FIRST AFRICAN-AMERICAN TO PLAY IN THE NBA. CHUCK COOPER WAS THE FIRST DRAFTED (BOSTON CELTICS) BUT LLOYD WAS THE FIRST TO ACTUALLY PLAY.

(SEE CHUCK COOPER ABOVE).

GEORGE GREGORY

GEORGE GREGORY WAS THE NATION'S FIRST BLACK ALL-AMERICAN BASKETBALL PLAYER WHO LATER WAS A NEW YORK CITY CIVIL SERVICE COMMISSIONER AND A CIVIC LEADER IN HARLEM. HE WAS THE CAPTAIN AND STAR CENTER OF THE COLUMBIA UNV. TEAM DURING THE 1930-31 SEASON WHEN THE SCHOOL WON IT'S FIRST CHAMPIONSHIP OF THE EASTERN INTERCOLLEGIATE LEAGUE (NOW KNOWN AS THE IVY LEAGUE).

(30)

HIGH SCHOOL MATCH QUIZ

IN 1974 MOSES MALONE WAS THE FIRST HIGH SCHOOL BASKETBALL PLAYER TO JUMP DIRECTLY FROM HIGH SCHOOL TO THE NATIONAL BASKETBALL ASSOCIATION. SINCE THEN THERE HAVE BEEN MANY OTHERS TO FOLLOW HIS LEAD.

LISTED ON THE LEFT ARE PLAYERS AND THE TEAM WHO DRAFTED THEM. CAN YOU MATCH THE PLAYER WITH THE HIGH SCHOOL, CITY AND STATE THEY WERE DRAFTED FROM ON THE RIGHT. INSERT LETTER IN THE SPACE PROVIDED.

MOSES MALONE

1. DARRYL DAWKINS
   PHILADELPHIA _____
2. KOBE BRYANT
   CHARLOTTE _____
3. TRACY McGRADY
   TORONTO _____
4. RASHARD LEWIS
   SEATTLE _____
5. KEVIN GARNETT
   MINNESOTA _____
6. DARIUS MILES
   L.A. CLIPPERS _____
7. LE BRON JAMES
   CLEVELAND _____
8. MONTA ELLIS
   GOLDEN STATE _____
9. ANDREW BYNUM
   L.A. LAKERS _____
10. JERMAINE O'NEAL
    PORTLAND _____

A. EVANS
   ERLANDO, FLA.
B. ELSIK
   AFIEF, TEXAS
C. FARRAGUT
   CHICAGO
D. LANIER
   JACKSON, MISS.
E. LOWES MERION
   ARDMORE, PA.
F. ST. JOSEPHS
   NEW JERSEY
G. EAST CLAIRE
   COLUMBIA, S.C.
H. MT. ZION ACADEMY
   DURHAM, N.C.
I. ST. VINCENT — ST. MARY
   AKRON, OHIO
J. EAST ST. LOUIS

LE BRON JAMES

TRACY McGRADY

KEVIN GARNETT

KOBE BRYANT

(31)

BASKETBALL'S
GOOD GUYS

DIKEMBE MUTOMBO

A SUCCESSFUL NBA CAREER HAS ALLOWED HIM TO ESTABLISH A FOUNDATION TO HELP IMPROVE THE HEALTH, EDUCATION AND QUALITY OF LIFE IN HIS HOMELAND, THE AFRICAN DEMOCRATIC REPUBLIC OF THE CONGO. HE GAVE THREE POINT FIVE MILLION TO ESTABLISH A NEW HOSPITAL THERE.

KEVIN JOHNSON

HE SPENT NEARLY ALL HIS STORIED NATIONAL BASKETBALL ASSOCIATION CAREER WITH THE PHOENIX SUNS (WHICH INCLUDES A OLYMPIC GOLD MEDAL WITH THE "DREAM TEAM")

HE FOUNDED ST. HOPE ACADEMY, A NON-PROFIT AFTER-SCHOOL EDUCATIONAL PROGRAM IN 1989, THE INITIAL PURPOSE TO TUTOR YOUNG PEOPLE-EVENTUALLY A $ MILLION DOLLAR 7,000 SQUARE FACILITY WAS BUILT.

A COMMUNITY DEVELOPMENT CORPORATION DESIGNED TO REVITAL-IZE INNER CITY COMMUNITIES GREW FROM IT, ALL WHICH INCLUDE A THEATER, BOOKSTORE, ART GALLERY, STARBUCKS AND LOFT APARTMENTS.

ST. HOPE PUBLIC SCHOOLS WAS FORMED, OPENING FIVE AUTO-MOMOUS SMALL CHARTER SCHOOLS ON THE CAMPUS OF SAC-RAMENTO HIGH SCHOOL (HIS ALMA MATER) ST. HOPE P.S. NOW PROVIDES MORE THAN 1,500 STUDENTS AT SACRAMENTO HIGH SCHOOL OPPORTUNITIES TO LEARN AT THE SCHOOL OF THE ARTS, BUSINESS, LAW HEALTH AND PUBLIC SERVICE

HE WAS ELECTED FIRST BLACK MAYOR OF SACRAMENTO.

EARLY BASKETBALL HISTORY
HARLEM RENAISSANCE

ROBERT DOUGLAS (COACH, OWNER, PLAYER) CREATED THE TEAM IN 1922. (THEY PLAYED THEIR FIRST GAME NOV. 30, 1923). THE OWNERS OF THE RENAISSANCE CASINO BALLROOM BECAME OWNERS OF THE TEAM. THE BALLROOM BECOMING HOME COURT, WITH DOUGLAS BEING RESPONSIBLE FOR SCHEDULING GAMES, TRAVEL, ETC.

ROBERT DOUGLAS

THE "RENS" CONTINUED PLAYING INTO THE 1940'S COMPLETING A RECORD OF 2,588 GAMES WON AND 529 LOST.

IN 1932 THEY WON 88 CONSECUTIVE GAMES INCLUDING THE FAMOUS CELTICS (WHITE TEAM). THEY BECAME THE FIRST BLACKS TO BE INDUCTED INTO THE BASKETBALL HALL OF FAME.

ROBERT DOUGLAS WAS ELECTED TO THE NAISMITH MEMORIAL BASKETBALL HALL OF FAME IN 1971.

THE HARLEM GLOBE TROTTERS
TEAM WAS FOUNDED IN 1952. OWNED AND COACHED BY ABE SAPERSTEIN OF CHICAGO. MANNIE JACKSON A FORMER GLOBE TROTTER BECAME THE FIRST BLACK TO OWN THE TEAM IN 1993.

Which Harlem
GLOBE TROTTER
is HE?

I STARTED PLAYING BASKETBALL AT LANGSTON UNIVERSITY (OKLAHOMA). MY COLLEGE TEAM COMPILED A 112-3 CAREER RECORD.

I WENT TO CHICAGO IN 1946 TO TRY OUT FOR THE HARLEM GLOBE TROTTERS. I CREATED AN UPROAR WITH MY DRIBBLING AND BALL HANDLING

I LATER FORMED MY OWN TEAM, "THE FABULOUS HARLEM MAGICIANS" IN 1953.

I TURNED DOWN OFFERS FROM THE MINNEAPOLIS LAKERS AND PHILADELPHIA WARRIORS. I REJOINED THE GLOBETROTTERS AS PLAYER COACH.

A.) "GOOSE" TATUM
B.) "SHOWBOAT" JONES
C.) MARQUES HAYNES

BASKETBALL HISTORY MAKERS

LEGEND SCRAMBLE QUIZ

CAN YOU UNSCRAMBLE THE NAMES OF
THESE LEGENDARY BASKETBALL PLAYERS?
USE CLUES TO HELP YOU

1.)

WILLIAM "POP" TEGAS

HE PLAYED FOR THE HARLEM RENAISSANCE AFTER HIGH SCHOOL IN NEW YORK CITY AND A BRIEF STAY AT CLAR UNIVERSITY IN ATLANTA.

HE SIGNED WITH THE ROCHESTER ROYALS OF THE NATIONAL BASKETBALL LEAGUE 1946-47 SEASON.

2.)

MEADOWLARK OMLEN

HE JOINED THE HARLEM GLOBE TROTTERS AFTER 2 YEARS IN ARMED SERVICES BRINGING HIS UNIQUE ABILITY TO COMBINE COMEDY AND WIZARDRY.

HE OWNED TEAM SUCH AS THE BUCKATEERS AND HARLEM STARS. HE PLAYED APPROXIMATELY IN 10,000 GAMES.

GLOBE TROTTER Legend

DON BARNETTE

KNOWN AS THE "DRIBBLING WIZARD" HE WAS THE FIRST BLACK PLAYER OFFERED A BASKETBALL SCHOLARSHIP TO MIAMI UNIVERSITY OF OHIO AFTER BEING CAPTAIN OF HIS MIDDLETOWN HIGH SCHOOL IN 1952 STATE CHAMPIONSHIP TEAM. THEY WON 26 GAMES AND LOST ONLY ONE.

WHILE SERVING IN THE U.S. NAVY HE AVERAGED 20 POINTS PER GAME AND MADE THE ALL-NAVY TEAM TWO STRAIGHT YEARS.

HE JOINED THE TROTTERS IN 1958 WHERE HE EARNED AFOREMENTIONED "DRIBBLING WIZARD" REPUTATION. DON PLAYED WITH THEM FOR FOUR YEARS.

HE WAS INDUCTED INTO THE BUTLER COUNTY SPORTS HALL OF FAME IN 1996 AND THE MIAMI UNIVERSITY HALL OF FAME IN 2000.

IN 2000 ANOTHER HONOR WAS AWARDED HIM WHEN HE ENTERED THE BLACK LEGENDS PRO-BASKETBALL HALL OF FAME.

3)

REECE "GOOSE" AUTMT

DISCOVERED BY ABE SAPERSTEIN, OWNER OF THE HARLEM GLOBE TROTTERS IN 1941, HE PLAYED FOR THE GLOBE TROTTERS FOR 12 SEASONS AS ONE OF THE BEST SHOWMAN OF ALL TIMES.

Full Court Quiz

Where did I go to school?

Can you tell where these basketballers went to college?
Circle the right answers

(1)

Derrick Rose

Chicago Bulls, Earned "Rookie of the Year" and in his 2nd season selected as an "All Star"
A) Mississippi State
B) Notre Dame
C) Memphis

(2)

Chamique Holdsclaw
She led her Queens, N.Y. high school team to 3 straight N.Y. State Championships
A) Duke
B) Tennessee
C) Florida State

(3)

Rebekkah Brunson
USA Women Team Cup winner, Olympics 2008 leading College rebounder

A) Georgia
B) Auburn
C) Tennessee

(4)

Demya Walker
New Jersey born, set rebound record average per game and most points in a season, named New Jersey's High School Athlete of the Year and Parade Magazine All-America 2nd team a high school senior she went on to star at:

A) Virginia
B) Alabama
C) South Carolina

(5)

Ruthie Bolton
Former college, Olympic and professional basketball player 1997-2004 with Sacramento Monarchs

A) LSU
B) Auburn
C) Colgate

Women's Basketball

Yolanda Griffith

Born in Chicago, she was named Parade Magazine's All- American Basketball Team in her senior year at GEO, Washington Carver High School.

She later attended Palm Beach Junior College in Florida, where she earned Junior College All-American Honors.

She played in the ABL and WNB leagues, she earned MVP. She was considered one of the greatest rebounder and defensive player in the history of women's basketball.

Women began playing basketball in 1882 less than a year after the game was invented

Kara Lawson

Shooting guard, who grew up in Washington D.C. won a Gold Medal at the 2008 Beijing Olympics. She attended the Univ. of Tennessee, receiving The Pomery Naismith award from the Women's Basketball Coaches Assn.

She turned pro with the Sacramento Monarchs the Connecticut Suns.

She won the Kim Perrot Sportsmanship award-2009

In the infancy of women's basketball when bloomers were introduced at sophie newcomb college

Nicole Powell

A Arizona native who became a standard basketball player at Stanford Univ. During her tenure there she broke many school records, was named an All – American three times.

She is to only female in Pac-10 history to have achieved multiple triple-double games. (10 or more in three different categories), during the same game.

Lisa Leslie

One of Women's early basketball pioneers. 3-time WNBA MVP and 4-time Olympic Gold Medal winner. She had a superb career at the Univ. of Southern CA. followed by 7 WNBA All-Star appearances and 2 WNBA championships over the course of 11 seasons with the Los Angeles Sparks.

The first official women's basketball game between two institutions took place between the university of California Berkeley and the Miss Head's school in the late 1800's.

(36)

Boxing

BOXING SCRAMBLE QUIZ

CAN YOU UNSCRAMBLE THE LAST NAME OF THESE NOTED BOXERS. USE THE CLUE BENEATH THEIR NAMES TO HELP YOU.

HISTORIC MOMENTS IN BOXING

1)

DICK GITRE

BORN IN NIGERIA, HE WON BOTH THE MIDDLE-WEIGHT AND LIGHT-HEAVYWEIGHT CHAMP-IONSHIPS AT DIFFERENT TIMES IN HIS CAREER.

NAME: _____

2)

THOMAS ARHNES

A WELTERWEIGHT TITLE-HOLDER WHO WAS NICK-NAMED THE "HIT MAN."
NAME: _____

JOE LOUIS

KNOCKED OUT MAX SCHMELING IN A 1938 FIGHT TO AVENGE AN EARLIER DEFEAT. WITH WORLD WAR II ON THE HORIZON AND NATION-ALISM AT ITS PEAK, SPONTANEOUS CELEBRATIONS ERUPTED WHEN LOUIS CRUSHED HIS GERMAN CHAL-LENGER IN THE FIRST ROUND.

JOE GANS
1874 – 1910

WAS THE FIRST AMER-ICAN-BORN AFRICAN-AMERICAN TO WIN A WORL CROWN (THE LIGHT WEIGHT) DEFE-ATING FRANK ERNE IN ONE ROUND.

THE AFTER STORY

BOTH JOE LOUIS AND MAX SCHMELING SERVED THEIR COUNTRIES IN THE ARMED FORCES DURING WORLD WAR II AND LOUIS WAS HIT WITH TAX PENALTIES THAT KEPT HIM FIGHTING LONGER THAN HE SHOULD HAVE. SCHMELING, WHO ONCE SHIELDED 2 JEWISH CHILDREN DURING A NAZI RAID, ADAPTED FROM NAZI PUPPET TO WESTERN CAPITALIST, OWNING A COCA-COLA BOTTLING PLANT IN POST WAR GERMANY.

SCHMELING EVEN HELPED LOUIS FINANCIALLY EVER SO OFTEN AFTER THEY BEGAN A FRIENDSHIP ON AN EPISODE OF THE TV SERIES "THIS IS YOUR LIFE" AND HELPED PAY FOR LOUIS' FUNERAL WHEN HE DIED IN 1981.

HUMOR IN HUE

"THE FIRST THING I WANT YOU TO DO IS TO FORGET ALL YOU'VE LEARNED ABOUT PASSIVE-RESISTANCE"

"JUST DON'T ASK HIM TO DEFINE 'BLACK POWER'!"

 **BOXING ONE QUIZ**

CAN YOU GUESS THE CORRECT ANSWERS TO THE QUESTIONS BELOW.

1.

FLOYD PATTERSON

HE BECAME HEAVY WEIGHT CHAMPION IN 1956. HE WAS GOLDEN GLOVE CHAMP, THEN EN WON A GOLD MEDAL ON THE OLYMPIC BOXING TEAM AT HELSINKI.

IN WHICH WEIGHT DIVISION?

A.) HEAVYWEIGHT
B.) LIGHT HEAVYWEIGHT
C.) MIDDLEWEIGHT

2.

SUGAR RAY ROBINSON

A 5 TIME MIDDLE WEIGHT CHAMPION WHO PREVIOUSLY HAD THE WELTERWEIGHT TITLE WAS CONSIDERED BY MANY TO BE THE BEST POUND FOR POUND BOXER IN HISTORY. HIS BIRTH NAME WAS:

A.) WALKER SMITH
B.) LOUIS BARROW
C.) ARNOLD CREAM

3.

MUHAMMAD ALI

A GOLD MEDAL WINNER IN THE LIGHT HEAVYWEIGHT BOXING DIVISION AT THE 1960 OLYMPICS IN ROME. HE UPSET SONNY LISTON IN SIX ROUNDS FOR THE HEAVYWEIGHT CHAMPIONSHIP IN 1964.

HE REFUSED INDUCTION INTO THE ARMED FORCES, AND WAS CONVICTED FOR DRAFT EVASION, LICENSE REVOKED AND STRIPPED OF HIS TITLE.
HE REGAINED HIS TITLE THREE TIMES.
HIS BIRTH NAME WAS:
A.) ARNOLD CREAM
B.) CASSIUS CLAY
C.) WALKER SMITH

TIGER FLOWERS 1895-1927 WAS THE FIRST BLACK MIDDLE WEIGHT CHAMP IN 1926 BEATING HARRY GREB.

4.

GEORGE "LITTLE CHOCOLATE" DIXON 1870-1909

HE BECAME THE FIRST BLACK WORLD CHAMPION IN BOXING WHEN HE WON THE BANTAM WEIGHT CHAMPIONSHIP JUNE 1890. WHERE WAS HE BORN?
A.) PARIS, FRANCE
B.) HARLEM, NEW YORK
C.) HALIFAX, NOVA SCOTIA

(39)

FIGHT KNIGHTS

JOHN HENRY LEWIS

FIGHTING OUT OF HIS HOMETOWN, OAKLAND, CALIFORNIA, HE WON THE LIGHT-HEAVYWEIGHT WORLD CHAMPIONSHIP IN 1935.

JOE JEANNETTE

A GREAT FIGHTER OF HIS ERA WHO FOUGHT THE GREAT JACK JOHNSON EIGHT TIMES.

MIKE TYSON

ONE OF THE YOUNGEST FIGHTERS TO WIN THE HEAVYWEIGHT CHAMPIONSHIP, BUT ONE OF THE MOST CONTROVERSIAL.

JOE FRAZIER

HIS FIGHTS WITH MUHAMMID ALI FOR THE WORLD'S HEAVYWEIGHT CHAMPIONSHIP WERE CLASSICS.

BOXING who am I?

I WAS BORN IN CUTHBERT, GA. ONE OF TWELVE CHILDREN. MOVED TO EASTON, PA. WHEN I WAS FIVE. QUIT SCHOOL AFTER 7TH GRADE TO HELP SUPPORT THE FAMILY.

WON THE NEW JERSEY AAU CHAMPIONSHIP

SERVED AS SPARRING PARTNER TO BOTH MUHAMMID ALI AND JOE FRAZIER

IN 1978 HE OUTBOXED KEN NORTON TO WIN WORLD BOXING COUNCIL HEAVYWEIGHT CHAMPIONSHIP

A. LEON SPINKS
B. MIKE WEAVER
C. LARRY HOLMES

Prize Fighter ✦ Quiz

CAN YOU SELECT THE RIGHT ANSWERS TO THE QUESTIONS ABOUT THE PRIZE FIGHTERS BELOW?

CIRCLE THE CORRECT ANSWERS

1)

SONNY LISTON

LOST HIS HEAVYWEIGHT TITLE TO MUHAMMAD ALI FEBRUARY 25, 1964. WHO DID HE WIN THE TITLE FROM ORIGINALLY?

A.) JOE WALCOTT
B.) EZZARD CHARLES
C.) FLOYD PATTERSON

2)

ANDRE WARD

AN OAKLAND, CA. RESIDENT WAS THE ONLY GOLD MEDAL WINNING BOXER AT THE 2004 ATHENS OLYMPIC GAMES. WHAT DIVISION DID HE WIN?

A.) LIGHT HEAVYWEIGHT
B.) HEAVY WEIGHT
C.) MIDDLE WEIGHT

3.)

EVANDER HOLYFIELD

A FOUR-TIME WORLD HEAVY-WEIGHT CHAMPION. IN A SECOND TITLE MATCH AGAINST MIKE TYSON, JUNE 1997 TYSON BIT OFF A BIT OF HIS:

A.) FINGER
B.) NOSE
C.) EAR

WHO AM I?

I HAD THREE CONTRO-VERSIAL BOXING MATCH-ES WITH MUHAMMAD ALI. THE LAST WAS A 15 ROUND LOSS IN 1976 WHICH MANY IN ATTENDANCE THOUGHT I HAD WON.

I WAS PROCLAIMED WORLD HEAVYWEIGHT CHAMPION BY THE WBC IN 1978.

MY SON KEN BECAME A PREMIER DEFENSIVE BACK FOR THE FOOTBALL S.F. 49ers. I AM:

A.) LEON SPINKS
B.) KEN NORTON
C.) LARRY HOLMES

Football

HALL OF FAME//BLACK COLLEGE ALUMNI Quiz

PICTURED BELOW ARE FOOTBALL PLAYERS WHO ATTENDED BLACK COLLEGES WHO WERE INDUCTED INTO THE PRO FOOTBALL HOME OF FAME AT THE END OF THEIR PLAYING CAREER. THEIR PLAYING POSITION AND TEAM APPEAR UNDER THEIR PICTURE. CAN YOU GUESS THE COLLEGE THEY ATTENDED. (CIRCLE RIGHT ANSWER).

1.)

WILLIE BROWN

OAKLAND RAIDERS DEFENSIVE BACK:

A.) MORGAN STATE

B.) LANGSTON

C.) GRAMBLING UNIVERSITY

2.)

DEACON JONES

DEFENSIVE LINEMAN LOS ANGELES RAMS 1961-1971, SAN DIEGO CHARGERS 1972-1973, WASHINGTON REDSKINS 1974:

A.) S.CAROLINA STATE - MISSISSIPPI VOCATIONAL
B.) JACKSON STATE

C.) PRAIRIE VIEW A&M

3.)

ROOSEVELT BROWN

NEW YORK GIANTS OFFENSIVE TACKLE 1953-1965

A.) S. CAROLINA STATE

B.) MORGAN STATE

C.) TUSKEGEE

CHARLES W. FOLLIS, NICKNAMED THE "BLACK CYCLONE", WAS THE FIRST BLACK TO PLAY PROFESSIONAL FOOTBALL—IN 1904 FOR THE SHELBY (OHIO) ATHLETIC CLUB

HE ALSO PLAYED PRO BASEBALL FOR THREE YEARS WITH THE CUBAN GIANTS

HEY! HE WAS THE FIRST BO JACKSON

SOUL CIRCLE

4-11   CHARLES W. FOLLIS

Hall of Fame Quiz Continued

MEL BLOUNT

CORNER BACK FOR THE PITTSBURGH STEELERS 1970 TO 1983:

A.) LINCOLN UNIVERSITY

B.) SOUTHERN UNIVERSITY

C.) FLORIDA A&M

KEN HOUSTON

STRONG SAFETY HOUSTON OILER 1967-1972-WASHINTON REDSKINS 1973-1980:

A.) ATLANTA UNIVERSITY

B.) TUSKEGEE

C.) PRAIRIE VIEW A&M

BUCK BUCHANAN

DEFENSIVE BACK KANSAS CITY CHIEFS 1963-1975:

A.) GRAMBLING UNIV.

B.) FISK UNIVERSITY

C.) SOUTHERN UNIV.

WILLIE LANIER

LINEBACKER, KANSAS CITY CHIEFS 1967-1977:

A.) MORGAN STATE

B.) ALABAMA A&M

C.) VIRGINIA UNION

LEM BARNEY

CORNERBACK, DETROIT LION 1967-1977

A.) DELAWARE STATE

B.) JACKSON STATE

C.) HAMPTON UNIVERSITY

LARRY LITTLE

SAN DIEGO CHARGERS 1967, MIAMI DOLPHINS 1969-1971 OFFENSIVE GUARD:

A.) TUSKEGEE

B.) MOREHOUSE UNIV.

C.) BETHUNE-COOKMAN COLLEGE

TAILBACK PUZZLE

J	H	F	J	N	O	T	Y	A	P	G	A
S	A	Y	E	R	K	Z	B	Y	E	L	H
X	B	C	A	G	X	I	H	D	F	L	C
D	I	C	K	E	R	S	O	N	B	E	D
C	O	K	M	S	R	E	G	O	R	B	P
G	A	L	I	M	O	R	E	C	O	P	Q
U	Q	R	A	Z	C	N	Y	A	P	M	J
X	E	N	O	S	P	M	I	S	W	A	D
T	B	R	H	U	E	S	A	Q	V	C	W
Y	O	U	N	G	G	A	R	R	E	T	T

EARL CAMPBELL
UNIV. OF TEXAS ALL-AMERICAN, HEISMAN TROPHY WINNER. NFL RUSHING CHAMPION—ENSHRINED IN FOOTBALL HALL OF FAME 1991

> CAN YOU FIND THE LAST NAMES OF THESE RUNNING BACKS IN THE ABOVE PUZZLE? NAMES APPEAR BACKWARDS, HORIZONTALLY, DIAGONALLY, VERTICALLY

ERIC DICKERSON
LOS ANGELES RAMS RUNNING BACK SET A RUSHING RECORD FOR A ROOKIE (1,808 YARDS) IN 1983 HIS SECOND YEAR HE INCREASED IT TO 2,150

BO JACKSON
STAR RUNNING BACK AT AUBURN UNIV. BEFORE BECOMING A 2-PRO SPORTS STAR. HITTING SPACE SHOT HOME RUNS FOR KANSAS CITY ROYALS AND TOUCHDOWN RUNS FOR THE LOS ANGELES RAIDERS

O. J. SIMPSON
HEISMAN TROPHY WINNER AT U.S.C. NUMBER ONE PICK OF THE BUFFALO BILLS IN 1973. HE SET A RECORD 2,003 YARDS GAINED IN A SEASON

Q.B. MATCH QUIZ

FOR MANY YEARS AFTER AFRICAN-AMERICANS WERE FINALLY ACCEPTED INTO PRO FOOTBALL, BLACK QUARTERBACKS WERE EXCLUDED. SOME OF THE QUARTERBACKS LISTED BELOW WERE AMONG THE FIRST TO PLAY THE POSITION AS PROFESSIONALS.

CAN YOU MATCH THE QUARTERBACKS (AT THE TOP) WITH THE TEAM THEY FIRST SIGNED WITH? (AT THE BOTTOM) INSERT THE RIGHT LETTER BESIDE THE QUARTERBACK.

QUARTERBACKS

1) MICHAEL VICK _____
2) DOUG WILLIAMS _____
3) JOE GILLIAM _____
4) DONOVAN McNABB _____
5) JAMES HARRIS _____
6) MARLIN BRISCOE _____
7) VINCE EVANS _____
8) WARREN MOON _____
9) STEVE McNAIR _____
10) DAUNTE CULPEPPER _____

TEAMS

A) TENNESSEE TITANS
B) MINNESOTA VIKINGS
C) HOUSTON OILERS
D) ATLANTA FALCONS
E) DENVER BRONCOS
F) PITTSBURGH STEELERS
G) BUFFALO BILLS
H) TAMPA BAY BUCCANEERS
I) PHILADELPHIA EAGLES
J) CHICAGO BEARS

JAMES HARRIS

MARLIN BRISCOE

DOUG WILLIAMS

VINCE EVANS

JOE GILLIAM

STEVE McNAIR

HEISMAN TROPHY QUIZ

LISTED ON THE LEFT ARE THE NAMES OF BLACK FOOTBALL PLAYERS WHO WERE AWARDED THE HEISMAN TROPHY (THE YEARS BEST PLAYER) ON THE RIGHT ARE NAMES OF THE UNIVERSITY THEY WERE ATTENDING WHEN THEY WON. CAN YOU MATCH THE PLAYER WITH HIS UNIVERSITY? PLACE THE CORRECT LETTER IN THE SPACE PROVIDED.

1. MARCUS ALLEN _____	A. NEBRASKA
2. TIM BROWN _____	B. GEORGIA
3. REGGIE BUSH _____	C. OKLAHOMA
4. EARL CAMPBELL _____	D. SOUTH CAROLINA
5. ERNIE DAVIS _____	E. U.S.C.
6. RON DAYNE _____	F. TEXAS
7. TONY DORSETT _____	G. WISCONSIN
8. MIKE GARRETT _____	H. NEBRASKA
9. GEORGE ROGERS _____	I. SYRACUSE
10. JOHNNY ROGERS _____	J. NOTRE DAME
11. MIKE ROZIER _____	K. PITTSBURGH
12. O.J. SIMPSON _____	
13. BILLY SIMS _____	
14. HERSCHEL WALKER _____	

* REGGIE BUSH

RON DAYNE

* BUSH HAD TO RETURN HIS TROPHY

TONY DORSETT

MARCUS ALLEN

BILLY SIMS

EARL CAMBELL

42

Pigskin Parade Quiz

CAN YOU COMPLETE THE LAST NAMES OF THE FOOTBALL PLAYERS PICTURED BELOW?

USE THE INFORMATION BELOW THE PICTURE TO AID YOU.

1.)

KENNY

`| | A | | | | | | |`

HE BROKE THE FOOTBALL PROFESSIONAL COLOR BARRIER IN 1946 WHICH WAS IN EXISTANCE SINCE 1935.

A LEGENDARY RUNNING BACK FOR UCLA. IN 1939 HE WAS UCLA'S FIRST ALL-AMERICAN. HE PLAYED 13 YEARS FOR THE L.A. RAMS.

2.)

EUGENE

`| | P | | | |`

HE WAS THE OAKLAND RAIDERS NUMBER ONE PICK OUT OF TEXAS A&I. EARNED ALL-LEAGUE HONORS AT GUARD INCLUDING BEING SELECTED TO THE PRO BOWL.

AFTER HIS PLAYING DAYS WERE OVER HE BECAME EXECUTIVE DIRECTOR OF THE NFL PLAYERS ASSOCIATION.

3.)

WOODY

`| | T | | | |`

HE WAS A SENSATIONAL OFFENSIVE AND DEFENSIVE PLAYER FOR UCLA. HE ALSO STARRED IN TRACK AS A DISCUS THROWER.

SIGNED BY LOS ANGELES RAMS IN 1946. LATER BECAME A MOVIE ACTOR.

WHAT IS THE REFEREE PENALIZING OUR QUARTERBACK FOR, GEORGE?

HE CALLED HIM FOR INTENTIONALLY GROUNDING, DIZ

11-5
MORRIE
©2004 CREATORS SYND. ALL RIGHTS RESERVED

I'VE BEEN INTENTIONALLY GROUNDED BY MY MOM MANY TIMES

LINEMAN QUIZ

CAN YOU SELECT THE RIGHT ANSWERS TO THE QUESTIONS ABOUT THE LINEMEN AND LINEBACKER PICTURED BELOW? CIRCLE THE CORRECT ANSWER BELOW.

1)

BOBBY BELL

ALL-STAR LINEBACKER FOR THE KANSAS CITY CHIEFS FOR 12 YEARS. HE WAS ALL-PRO FOR 8 YEARS. DRAFTED OUT OF MINNESOTA, WHAT TROPHY DID HE WIN IN COLLEGE

A.) OUTLAND TROPHY

B.) MOST VALUABLE PLAYER

C.) ROOKIE OF THE YEAR

2)

JIM PARKER

HE EXCELLED ON DEFENSE AT OHIO STATE, BECAME ONE OF THE MOST EFFECTIVE OFFENSIVE LINEMAN IN PRO BALL. HIS BLOCKING PROTECTED WHICH LENGENDARY QUARTERBACK:

A.) JOHN BRODIE

B.) JOHNNY UNITAS

C.) Y.A. TITTLE

HE WAS FIRST OFFENSIVE LINEMAN INDUCTED INTO HALL OF FAME -1973

3)

BILL WILLIS

HE WON HIS JOB WITH THE CLEVELAND BROWN ON A TRY-OUT. HE MADE THE SAVING TACKLE IN THE TITLE GAME AGAINST THE N.Y. GIANTS AFFORDING CLEVELAND IT'S FIRST N.F.L. TITLE THEIR INITIAL SEASON. HE PLAYED BOTH WAYS (OFFENSE AND DEFENSE) IN COLLEGE.

A.) FISK

B.) NEBRASKA

C.) OHIO STATE

HE WAS INDUCTED INTO PRO FOOTBALL HALL OF FAME IN 1977.

4)

LAWRENCE TAYLOR

AN ALL-PRO DEVASTATING LINE BACKER PLIED HIS TRADE FOR :
A.) N.Y. GIANTS
B.) N.Y. JETS
C.) GREEN BAY PACKERS

Football Scramble Quiz

CAN YOU UNSCRAMBLE THE NAMES OF THESE NOTED FOOTBALL PLAYERS THROUGHOUT HISTORY? USE THE INFORMATION UNDER THEIR PICTURES TO AID YOU.

1)

GALE
YARSES

A RUNNING BACK FOR THE CHICAGO BEARS, WHO IN 1965 SCORED 6 TOUCH-DOWNS IN ONE GAME AGAINST THE S.F. 49ers. HE SCORED A ROOKIE RECORD 22 TDS, 135 POINTS AS PLAYER OF THE GAME IN 3 PRO BOWLS. ENSHRINED IN FOOTBALL HALL OF FAME, 1977.

2)

MARION
TEYOML

PLAYING FULLBACK FOR CLEVELAND BROWNS OF THE NEW ALL AMERICAN CONFERENCE TEAM THAT HE JOINED IN 1946. HE HELPED LEAD THE TEAM TO MULTIPLE TITLES. HE PLAYED BOTH ON OFFENSE AND LINE BACKER ON DEFENSE.

3)

LEN
RDOF

HE WAS CHOSEN ALL-AMERICAN END WHILE PLAYING FOR MICHIGAN, IN-CLUDING 1947 ROSE BOWL. JOINED THE CLEVELAND BROWNS IN 1950 AS A DEFENSIVE EARNING ALL-PRO HONORS AND ENSHRINED INTO HALL OF FAME 1976.

WHO AM I?

I HELPED THE SAN FRAN-CISCO 49ers WIN 3 SUPER BOWLS. ALONG THE WAY I WAS NAMED MVP OF SUPER BOWL XXIII AND BECAME THE MOST PROLIFIC PASS RECEIVER IN NFL HISTORY DURING MY CAREER WITH THE 49ers, OAKLAND RAID-ERS AND SEATTLE SEA HAW-KS. HE SET LEAGUE MARKS FOR RECEPTIONS, YARDS RECEIVING, TOUCHDOWNS, TOUCHDOWN RECEPTIONS AND CONSECUTIVE GAMES PLAYED WITH AT LEAST ONE CATCH.
A.) WOODY STRODE
B.) JERRY RICE
C.) TIM BROWN

Profile *of a* **LEGEND**

OLLIE MATSON

AN ALL-AMERICAN RUNNING BACK AT THE UNIVERSITY OF SAN FRANCISCO. HE WON A BRONZE MEDAL IN THE 400 METER RACE AT THE HELSINKI OLYMPIC GAMES IN 1952 AND A SILVER MEDAL AS A MEMBER OF THE USA 1600 METER RELAY TEAM.

HE WAS PRO ROOKIE OF THE YEAR PLAYING FOR THE N.F.L. CARDINALS.

THE LOS ANGELES RAMS TRADED NINE PLAYERS FOR HIM.

HE WAS NAMED ALL-PRO FOUR YEARS AND WAS INDUCTED INTO THE PRO-FOOTBALL HALL OF FAME IN 1972.

WILLIE JEFFRIES

BECAME HEAD COACH AT WICHITA STATE IN 1979 TO BECOME THE 1st BLACK HEAD COACH AT A MAJOR WHITE INSTITUTION.

Who Are They?
CIRCLE THE RIGHT ANSWER

1.)

THE FIRST BLACK QB TO PLAY (AND WIN) IN THE SUPER BOWL, PLAYING FOR THE WASHINGTON REDSKINS. HE WON MVP AWARD FOR SUPER BOWL XXII.

A.) STEVE McNAIR

B.) JOE GILLIAM

C.) DOUG WILLIAMS

2.)

HE SIGNED A FOOTBALL CONTRACT IN 1904 WITH A SHELBY OHIO TEAM BECOMING THE FIRST BLACK PRO FOOTBALL PLAYER.

A.) CHARES W. FOLLIS

B.) FRED "DUKE" SLATER

C.) RAY KEMP

3.)

A STAR OF THE 1950'S HIS NICK-NAME WAS "NIGHT TRAIN" AFTER SERVICE IN THE ARMY, SIGNED BY THE L.A. RAMS AFTER A TRYOUT HE BECAME A LEADING DEFENSIVE BACK, INTERCEPTING A RECORD 14 PASSES IN HIS ROOKIE SEASON IN A 12 GAME SCHEDULE. ENSHRINED IN THE FOOTBALL HALL OF FAME IN 1974.

A.) LEN FORD

B.) MIKE GARRETT

C.) DICK LANE

Super RUNNING BACKS

WILLIE GALIMORE

AFTER A SUCCESSFUL CAREER AT FLORIDA A&M HE HAD A STARRING CAREER WITH THE CHICAGO BEARS WHICH WAS CUT SHORT WHEN HE WAS KILLED IN A 1964 AUTO ACCIDENT.

GALE SAYERS

CHICAGO BEARS 1965 NFL SCORING CHAMPION AND "ROOKIE OF THE YEAR"
ENSHRINED INTO PRO FOOTBALL HALL OF FAME - 1977.

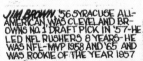

CLAUDE "BUDDY" YOUNG

FIVE-FOOT-FOUR-AND-ONE HALF INCH, 160 POUNDS WITH NEW YORK YANKEES, RUSHED FOR 1,275 YARDS AND 703 YARDS PASS CATCHING. HE LATER BECAME NFL DIRECTOR OF PUBLIC RELATIONS. HE WAS KILLED IN AN AUTOMOBILE ACCIDENT.

MIKE GARRETT

IN 3 YEARS AT USC HE GAINED 4,876 NET YARDS RUSHING, PASSING RECEIVING, PUNT RETURNS AND KICKOFF RETURNS. HE WON THE HEISMAN TROPHY IN 1965.
HE BECAME USC ATHLETIC DIRECTOR.

JIM BROWN, '56 SYRACUSE ALL-AMERICAN, WAS CLEVELAND BROWNS NO.1 DRAFT PICK IN '57 - HE LED NFL RUSHERS 8 YEARS - HE WAS NFL-MVP 1958 AND '65 AND WAS ROOKIE OF THE YEAR 1957

HE GAINED 12,312 YARDS RUSHING, 262 RECEPTIONS, 15,459 COMBINED NET YDS AND 756 POINTS SCORED

HE SHOULDA CALLED A CAB FOR AT LEAST SOME OF THAT DISTANCE

SOUL CIRCLE

JIM BROWN

TAIL BACK PUZZLE

YOU ARE A LINEBACKER ASSIGNED TO STOP THE RUNNING BACK (OR TAIL BACK) BUT FIRST YOU MUST FIND THE RUNNER BEFORE STOPPING HIM. IN THE FOLLOWING PAGE, TRY TO FIND THE LAST NAME OF THE TAIL BACKS LISTED BELOW. NAMES APPEAR HORIZONTAL, VERTICAL, BACKWARDS AND ON A SLANT.

TONY
• DORSETT
PITTSBURGH RUNNING BACK STAR, THEN A STAR FOR THE DALLAS COWBOYS.

JOE "THE JET"
PERRY •
IN 1956 HE BECAME THE FIRST TO GAIN 1000 YARDS. HE PLAYED FOR 49ers AND COLTS OVER A 14 YEAR CAREER.

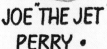

EMMITT SMITH •
DALLAS COWBOY RUNNING BACK BECAME THE NFL'S ALL TIME RUSHING LEADER.

I'D LOVE TO PLAY IN THE BACKFIELD WITH *WALTER PAYTON* THE CHICAGO BEARS GREAT HALL-OF-FAME RUNNING BACK – A JACKSON STATE STAR – HIS

JERSEY, NUMBER "34" WAS RETIRED WHEN HIS PLAYING DAYS WERE OVER – HE WAS NICKNAMED "SWEETNESS" DUE TO HIS RUNNING STYLE

IF YOU GUYS PLAYED TOGETHER, YOU WOULD BE KNOWN AS "SWEET AND SOUR"

9-23

SOUL CIRCLE

WALTER PAYTON

Name the ballcarrier Quiz

CAN YOU COMPLETE THE LAST NAME OF THE FOOTBALL PLAYERS PICTURED BELOW? USE THE CLUES UNDER THE PICTURES

1)

JOHN HENRY

| | G | | N | | O | |

A FORMER PITTSBURGH (CA) HIGH SCHOOL STAR FULLBACK, PLAYED PRO BALL WITH S.F. 49ers AND THE PITTSBURGH STEELERS. HE WAS THEIR NUMBER TWO DRAFT PICK IN 1953. HE WAS ENSHRINED IN THE NATIONAL FOOTBALL LEAGUE HALL OF FAME IN 1987

2)

JEROME "BRUD"

| H | | | | | | |

HE WAS ALL-AMERICAN END ON CORNELL'S BIG RED FOOTBALL TEAM IN THE 1930s, THE FIRST BLACK ATHLETE TO DO SO. HE WAS THE PREMIER END OF HIS DAY.
IN 1970 HE WAS APPOINTED AMBASSADOR TO SWEEDEN

3)

MARCUS

| | L | | | |

VERSATILE RUNNING BACK-HEISMAN TROPHY WINNER FOR U.S.C. SETTING ALL TIME RUSHING RECORD NAMED ROOKIE OF THE YEAR AND ALL PRO HIS FIRST YEAR WITH THE LOS ANGELES RAIDERS, NAMED MVP OF SUPER BOWL XVIII

4)

CLEM

| | | N | | | | |

HE PLAYED SEVEN SEASONS (1961-1967) WITH THE OAKLAND RAIDERS AFTER STARRING AT PRAIRIE VIEW COLLEGE. HE RUSHED FOR 5,103 AS A RAIDER AND FROM 1962 TO 1967 HE WAS THE CLUB'S LEADING RUSHER. IN 1963, HE RUSHED FOR TWO HUNDRED YARDS AGAINST THE NEW YORK JETS

Running Back Quiz

CAN YOU CHECK THE RIGHT ANSWERS
TO THE QUESTIONS ABOUT THESE NOTED
FOOTBALL RUNNING BACKS

1)

JOHNNY ROGERS

PLAYING FOR NEBRASKA, OPERATING AS A PUNT RETURNER, PASS RECEIVER AND RUNNING BACK. I BROKE MANY OFFENSIVE RECORDS IN MY THREE YEAR CAREER, AND LATER HAD AN OUTSTANDING CAREER IN THE PRO'S WITH THE CANADIAN FOOTBALL LEAGUE AND THE SAN DIEGO CHARGERS.

WHAT PRESTIGIOUS TROPHY DID I WIN?

A) MOST VALUABLE PLAYER

B) OUTLAND TROPHY

C) HEISMAN TROPHY

2)

WALTER PAYTON

CHICAGO BEARS GREAT RUNNING BACK RUSHED OVER 1000 YARDS IN 10 OF HIS 13 SEASONS BECOMING NFL'S TOP GROUND GAINER, TOTALLING 16,726 YARDS. HIS NUMBER 34 JERSEY WAS RETIRED BY THE BEARS. HE WAS ENSHRINED IN PRO-FOOTBALL'S HALL OF FAME 1993.

WHICH BLACK COLLEGE DID HE ATTEND AND PLAY FOOTBALL FOR?

A) JACKSON STATE

B) TEXAS SOUTHERN

C) FISK UNIVERSITY

RUNNING BACK WHO AM I?

I WAS A RUNNING BACK FOR SYRACUSE AND MY TEAM'S LEADING GROUND GAINER FOR 3 SEASONS. I WON THE HEISMAN TROPHY IN 1961, THE FIRST BLACK ATHLETE TO BE SO HONORED. AFTER GRADUATION I SIGNED WITH THE CLEVELAND BROWNS FOR THE THEN ASTRONOMICAL SUM OF 80,000 DOLLARS. I WAS STRUCK DOWN WITH LEUKEMIA, POSTHUMOUSLY ELECTED TO THE PRO FOOTBALL HALL OF FAME.

A) JIM BROWN

B) ERNIE DAVIS

C) O.J. SIMPSON

"YOU'VE HEARD OF 'TOO-TALL JONES'? WELL MEET 'TOO SHORT MIKKI'!"

"I'VE BEEN TRADED TO THE 'TENTH STREET TIGERS' FOR SIX MARBLES A JACK KNIFE AND AN AUTOGRAPHED PHOTO OF ROGER GODELL"

"IT MEANS THE 'SOCIETY FOR THE PREVENTION OF QUARTERBACK SACKS!'"

BRAIN GAME

MANY ATHLETES GAINED EVEN MORE FAME AFTER THEY LEFT THE PLAYING FIELD. PICTURED BELOW ARE SOME SUCH ATHLETES. CAN YOU GUESS WHO THEY ARE BY READING THE CLUES? CIRCLE THE RIGHT ANSWER

1.)

ONE OF PRO FOOTBALL'S GREATEST OLD TIME TACKLES. HE WON ALL-AMERICAN HONORS AT IOWA, PLAYED OFFENSE AND DEFENSE. TURNED PRO IN 1922. FIRST BLACK ELECTED TO PRO FOOTBALL'S HALL OF FAME.

HE PRACTICE LAW FOR TWO DECADES. ELECTED TO THE BENCH IN CHICAGO IN 1948 AND REMAINED A JUDGE THE REST OF HIS LIFE.

FRED "DUKE"

| S | | | | |

2.)

TWICE ALL-AMERICAN END. HELD 15 VARSITY LETTERS IN FOOTBALL, BASEBALL, BASKETBALL AND TRACK. TOP STUDENT IN 1919 CLASS OF RUTGERS UNIVERSITY WHERE HE WON PHI BETA KAPPA HONORS. HE RECEIVED HIS LAW DEGREE FROM COLUMBIA UNIVERSITY.

HE BECAME AN ACTOR, WAS A SINGER AND AN ACTIVIST.

PAUL
| | | | E | | | |

3.)

A NEW JERSEY NATIVE, HE STARTED HIS BASEBALL CAREER PITCHING FOR THE BALTIMORE ELITE GIANTS IN THE NEGRO LEAGUES, AT MORGAN COLLEGE, THEN THE BROOKLYN DODGERS.

AFTER RETIREMENT HE EVENTUALLY BECAME VICE-PRESIDENT OF GREYHOUND CORP.

JOE
| B | | | | |

4.)

WHEN HE PLAYED DEFENSIVE TACKLE FOR THE MINNESOTA VIKINGS HE ATTENDED LAW SCHOOL IN THE OFF SEASON.

HE WAS A NINE-TIME ALL PRO AND INDUCTED INTO THE HALL OF FAME. HE BECAME ASSISTANT ATTORNEY GENERAL OF MINNESOTA.

ALAN
| A | | | |

Track & Field

HISTORIC events IN TRACK & FIELD

AUGUST, 1936
OLYMPIC GAMES
BERLIN, GERMANY

JESSE OWENS

WON 4 GOLD MEDALS (100 AND 200 METER DASHES, LONG JUMP AND 400 METER RELAY) SMASHING OLYMPIC RECORDS NINE TIMES (IN PRELIMINARY RACES). ADOLF HITLER REFUSED TO ACKNOW — LEDGE HIM AND THE MEDALS HE WON.

EARLIER IN THE BIG 10 CHAMPION — SHIP IN ANN ARBOR, MICHIGAN. ON MAY 25, 1935 HE SET 5 WORLD RECORDS AND TIED A SIXTH WITHIN 45 MINUTES.

TRACK and FIELD SCRAMBLE

CAN YOU UNSCRAMBLE THE NAMES OF THE TRACK AND FIELD STARS PICTURED BELOW. USE THE INFORMATION UNDER THE PICTURE TO AID YOU. (ONLY LAST NAMES SCRAMBLED).

1.

ARCHIE
LIAIWLSM

A UNIVERSITY OF CAL-IFORNIA (BERKELEY) RUNNER, AN UPSET VICTOR IN THE 1936 OLYMPICS IN GERMANY.

2.

MILT
LMAECBL

HE WON THE OLYMPIC DECATHLON GOLD MEDAL IN 1956 AT MELBOURNE, AUSTRALIA.

3.

HOWARD P.
WRED

HE WON THE NATIONAL TITLE IN THE 100 YARD DASH IN 1912 AND 1913 AND THE NATIONAL TITLE IN THE 220 YARD DASH IN 1913.

PROFILE
of a Legend

CARL LEWIS

AT THE 1996 OLYMPICS IN ATLANTA, HE WON HIS RECORD SETTING FOURTH STRAIGHT GOLD LONG JUMP MEDAL AND RECORD TYING NINTH GOLD MEDAL IN OLYMPIC COMPETITION, EQUALING THE STANDARD SET BY FINNISH LONG DISTANCE STAR PAAVO NURMI 70 YEARS EARLIER.

HIS WINS WERE IN THE 100 AND 200 METER DASH, 400 METER RELAY AS WELL AS THE LONG JUMP.

HIS OLYMPIC CAREER STARTED AT THE LOS ANGELES GAMES IN 1984 WHERE HE EQUALED JESSE OWENS 1936 BERLIN OLYMPIC RECORD, WINNING THE 100, 200 METER RACES, 400 METER RELAY AND LONG JUMP.

WHO ARE THEY?

① IN THE 1992 OLYMPIC GAMES IN BARCELONA SHE LOST THE EVENT SHE WAS SUPPOSED TO WIN (110 METER HURDLES) AND WON THE EVENT SHE WASN'T SUPPOSED TO, THE (100 METER DASH).

A.) GWEN TORRENCE

B.) GAIL DEVERS

C.) JULIET CUTHBERT

② HE FAILED TO QUALIFY IN HIS FAVORITE EVENT, THE 110 HURDLES FOR THE 1948 OLYMPICS IN LONDON, THEREFORE WENT AS A SPRINTER. HE WAS AN UPSET WINNER IN THE 100 METERS IN A RECORD SETTING 10.3.

FOUR YEARS LATER AT HELSINKI HE WON THE OLYMPIC 110 HURDLES IN RECORD BREAKING 13.7

A.) LEE CALHOUN

B.) WILLIE DAVENPORT

C.) HARRISON DILLARD

MEMORABLE MOMENTS IN TRACK & FIELD

FRANKLIN JACOBS

HE SET THE WORLD'S INDOOR HIGH JUMP RECORD AT 7'-7¼"

BOB BEAMON

BREAKS THE WORLD OLYMPIC LONG JUMP RECORD 29 FT. 2½ INCHES BETTERING THE RECORD BY ALMOST 2 FEET. (MEXICO CITY 1968)

JAVIER SOTOMAYOR

FROM CUBA. HE WAS THE FIRST TO CLEAR 8 FT. IN THE HIGH JUMP.

STEVE LEWIS

A FORMER FREMONT HIGH SCHOOLER, WINNER OF THE STATE MEET, WINS THE 400 METER RACE IN AN UPSET WIN AT THE SEOUL, SOUTH KOREA OLYMPICS MAKING HIM, A 19 YEAR OLD, THE THE YOUNGEST GOLD MEDAL WINNER SINCE 1908.

YOU GOTTA HAVE HEART TO WIN AN OLYMPIC GOLD MEDAL, RANDY

YOU MEAN DE HART! DE HART HUBBARD

HE BECAME THE FIRST AFRICAN AMERICAN TO WIN A GOLD MEDAL WHEN HE WON THE LONG JUMP IN 1924

OKAY, BUT YOU GOTTA HAVE DE TALENT, TOO!

MORRIE

SOUL CIRCLE

7-13

DE HART HUBBARD

4)

RALPH METCALFE

HE WINS SILVER MEDAL IN 100 METER DASH IN 1932 BEHIND EDDIE TOLAND IN THE LOS ANGELES OLYMPICS SECOND AGAIN IN 1936 OLYMPICS IN GERMANY BEHIND JESSE OWENS. HE WON GOLD IN 1936 IN THE 4 X 100 RELAY.

LATER HE BECAME:

A.) MAILMAN

B.) DOCTOR

C.) CONGRESSMAN

5)

RAFER JOHNSON

HE WON SILVER MEDAL IN IN DECATHLON AT THE 1956 OLYMPICS IN MELBOURNE, RETURNED IN 1960 TO WIN THE GOLD IN THE EVENT IN THE ROME OLYMPICS. EARLIER HE WAS AWARDED A SCHOLARSHIP TO U.C.L.A. AFTER A SENSATIONAL HIGH SCHOOL CAREER IN:

A.) BARSTOW, CA.

B.) KINGSBURG, CA.

C.) BAKERSFIELD, CA.

6)

ABEBE BIKILA

HE WON CONSECUTIVE OLYMPIC MARATHONS (1960 & 1964) RUNNING BAREFOOT.

HIS OCCUPATION IN HIS HOME COUNTRY OF ETHIOPIA WAS:

A.) PALACE GARDENER

B.) PALACE GUARD

C.) PALACE CHEF

WILLIE DAVENPORT AND **JEFF GADLEY** WERE THE FIRST AFRICAN-AMERICANS TO PARTICIPATE IN THE WINTER OLYMPIC GAMES - 1984

TRACK & FIELD

WHO AM I?

I WON GOLD MEDALS IN THE 1948 AND 1952 OLYMPICS IN THE 800 METER EVENT. I WON ANOTHER GOLD MEDAL IN THE 4×400 METER RELAY IN THE 1948 OLYMPICS ALONG WITH A BRONZE MEDAL IN THE 400 METER EVENT.

IN THE 1952 OLYMPICS, BESIDES THE GOLD MEDAL, I WON A SILVER MEDAL IN THE 4×400 RELAY.

I WON THE JAMES E. SULLIVAN MEMORIAL AWARD AS TOP AMATEUR ATHLETE IN THE U.S. AND WAS ELECTED TO THE U.S. OLYMPIC HALL OF FAME.

I SERVED AS SPORTS AMBASSADOR IN AFRICA WHERE I PROVIDED TRAINING RESPONSIBLE FOR THE EMERGANCE OF THE AFRICAN DISTANCE RUNNER. I AM _ _ _ _ _

A.) JOHN WOODRUFF
B.) MAL WHITFIELD
C.) JOHN BORICAN

AT THE 1932 OLYMPIC GAMES IN LOS ANGELES, *EDDIE TOLAN* BECAME THE FIRST AFRICAN-AMERICAN ATHLETE TO WIN...

THE 100-METER OLYMPIC SPRINT BY A HAIR'S BREATH AHEAD OF RALPH MEDCALFE

WHATEVER HAPPENED TO THE HARE?

SOUL CIRCLE

EDDIE TOLAN

OLYMPIC GAMES QUIZ-Z-Z

CAN YOU SELECT THE RIGHT ANSWERS ABOUT THE TRACK AND
FIELD OLYMPIC MEDALIST PICTURED BELOW?
CIRCLE THE RIGHT ANSWER.

1.)

RALPH BOSTON

MANY TIMES HOLDER OF THE LONG
JUMP RECORD AND MEMBER OF
THE '60,'64 AND '68 OLYMPIC TEAM.
HE BROKE THE OLYMPIC LONG
JUMP RECORD PREVIOUSLY HELD
BY:

A.) BOB BEAMON

B.) WILLIE STEELE

C.) JESSE OWENS

2.)

CHARLES DUMAS

A COMPTON JUNIOR COLLEGE STAR
AND 1956 OLYMPIC GOLD MEDAL
WINNER. HE WAS THE FIRST ATHLETE
TO :

A.) HIGH JUMP 7 FT.

B.) LONG JUMP 27 FT.

C.) POLE VAULT 15 FT.

3.)

RAFER JOHNSON

WON THE GOLD MEDAL IN THE DE-
CATHLON IN THE 1960 OLYMPICS
IN ROME AFTER WINNING SILVER
IN MELBORNE IN 1956.
WHO WON THE EVENT IN '56?

A.) WILLIAM TOOMEY

B.) BRUCE JENNER

C.) MILTON CAMPBELL

RALPH MEDCALFE FINISHED
SECOND IN THE 100-METER
DASH IN THE OLYMPIC GAMES
OF 1932 IN LOS ANGELES AND
AGAIN IN 1936 (LOSING TO
JESSE OWENS) IN BERLIN.

HE WAS LATER
TO BE ELECTED
TO CONGRESS.

FINALLY
WON ONE,
EH ?

I WOULDN'T
SAY THAT!

MOORE
7-18

SOUL
CIRCLE

RALPH MEDCALFE

SPRINTER *Quiz*

CIRCLE THE CORRECT ANSWERS TO THESE QUESTIONS ABOUT THE OLYMPIC GAMES RUNNERS.

1.)

LEE EVANS

HE RAN A WORLD RECORD 43.8 400 METERS AT THE 1968 OLYMPICS IN MEXICO. WHICH UNIVERSITY DID HE COMPETE FOR.

A. S.F. CITY COLLEGE

B. SAN JOSE STATE

C. UNIVERSITY OF SAN FRANCISCO

2.)

JOHN WOODRUFF

HE BECAME THE FIRST AFRICAN-AMERICAN ATHLETE TO WIN THE OLYMPIC GAMES COMPETITION SINCE 1912 WHEN HE WON THE 1936 EVENT IN GERMANY. HE WAS KNOWN TO HAVE A STRIDE OF:

A. 8 FT. 9 INCHES

B. 9 FT. 7 INCHES

C. 9 FT. 5 INCHES

WHO AM I? II

I WAS THE FIRST BLACK TO COMPETE IN THE OLYMPIC GAMES.
I FINISHED FOURTH IN THE 400 METER DASH AND THIRD IN THE 400 HURDLES IN THE 1904 GAMES.
I ATTENDED THE UNIVERSITY OF WISCONSIN.

A. DE HART HUBBARD

B. JUIN WOODRUFF

C. GEORGE POAGE

3.)

MICHAEL JOHNSON

IN THE 1996 OLYMPIC GAMES IN ATLANA, GEORGIA HE BECAME THE FIRST MALE ATHLETE TO:

A.) WIN GOLD MEDALS IN BOTH THE 200 AND 400 METERS.

B.) SET 2 WORLD RECORD IN 2 EVENTS.

C.) WIN GOLD MEDALS IN THE 400 AND 800 METERS.

JOHN BAXTER "DOC" TAYLOR JR. (1882-1908)
BECAME THE FIRST BLACK WINNER OF AN OLYMPIC GOLD MEDAL (FOR THE 4 × 400 RELAY IN LONDON IN 1908).
HE DIED 5 MONTHS LATER.

Record Makers and Breakers

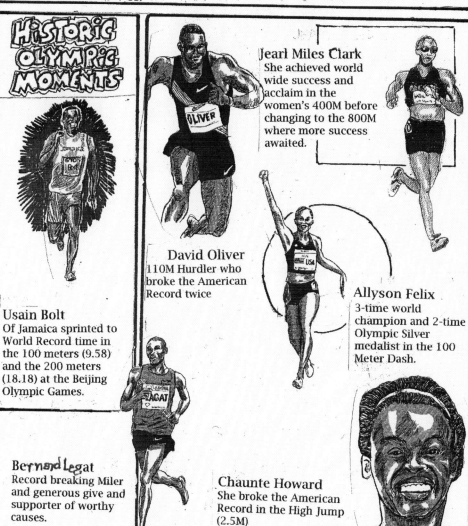

Historic Olympic Moments

Usain Bolt
Of Jamaica sprinted to World Record time in the 100 meters (9.58) and the 200 meters (18.18) at the Beijing Olympic Games.

Jearl Miles Clark
She achieved world wide success and acclaim in the women's 400M before changing to the 800M where more success awaited.

David Oliver
110M Hurdler who broke the American Record twice

Allyson Felix
3-time world champion and 2-time Olympic Silver medalist in the 100 Meter Dash.

Bernard Legat
Record breaking Miler and generous give and supporter of worthy causes.

Chaunte Howard
She broke the American Record in the High Jump (2.5M)

MIKE POWELL

LONG JUMPS 29-4½ AUG. 1991 IN TOKYO, BREAKING RECORD SET IN 1968.

EULACE PEACOCK

A TEMPLE UNIVERSITY SPRINTER OF THE 1930's AND FRIEND OF JESSE OWEN. HE DEFEATED OWENS FIVE TIMES IN NINE MONTHS IN 1935, A HAMSTRING INJURY PREVENTED HIM FROM MAKING THE 1936 UNITED STATES OLYMPIC TEAM.

BOB HAYES

HE WON THE 100 METER DASH AT THE 1964 OLYMPICS IN TOKYO THEN WENT ON TO BECOME A STAR WIDE RECEIVER FOR THE DALLAS COWBOY OF THE NATIONAL FOOTBALL LEAGUE

MAURICE GREENE

HE HELD THE 100 METER RECORD AT 9.79 AND CAPTURED THE 2000 OLYMPIC GOLD MEDAL IN THE EVENT AT CIDNEY

LEE CALHOUN

HE WON TWO OLYMPIC GOLD MEDALS FOR THE 110 METER HURDLES IN MELBOURE IN 1956 AND AGAIN IN ROME IN 1960

ANDY STANFIELD

HE WON THE 200 METER AND GOLD IN THE 400 METER RELAY AT THE 1956 MELBOURNE OLYMPICS

TRACK QUIZ

CAN YOU ANSWER THESE QUESTIONS REGARDING THESE TRACK STARS? CIRCLE THE CORRECT ANSWER.

1.)

DE HART HUBBARD

WAS THE FIRST AFRICAN-AMERICAN TO WIN AN OLYMPIC GOLD MEDAL IN 1924. HE WON THE:

A.) LONG JUMP

B.) 100 METER DASH

C.) HIGH JUMP

2.)

BEN JOHNSON

OF CANADA WON THE 1988 100 METER OLYMPIC FINALS 9.79 SECONDS. HE WAS STRIPPED OF HIS GOLD MEDAL FOR HAVING ANABOLIC STEROIDS IN HIS SYSTEM AND DISQUALIFIED. THE GOLD MEDAL THEN WENT TO: USA'S

A.) DENNIS MITCHELL

B.) CARL LEWIS

C.) BOB HAYES

3.)

ALICE COACHMAN

THE FIRST BLACK WOMAN TO WIN AN OLYMPIC GOLD MEDAL (1948). SHE WON:

A.) HIGH JUMP · B.) LONG JUMP · C.) 100 MTR. DASH

EVENT MATCH QUIZ

OLYMPIC GOLD MEDAL WINNERS AND THE YEAR THEY COMPETED ARE LISTED BELOW. CAN YOU MATCH THE NAME WITH HIS EVENT LOCATED AT THE BOTTOM. PLACE CORRECT LETTER IN SPACE PROVIDED.

1. JOHN WOODRUFF 1936 _____
2. CHARLIE DUMAS 1956 _____
3. WILLIE STEELE 1948 _____
4. ANDY STANFIELD 1952 _____
5. BOB HAYES 1964 _____
6. CHARLIE JENKINS 1956 _____
7. WILLIE DAVENPORT 1968 _____
8. MILT CAMPBELL 1956 _____

— EVENT —

A. 200 METER
B. 100 METER
C. 400 METER
D. 800 METER
E. 110 METER HURDLE
F. DECATHLON
G. LONG JUMP
H. HIGH JUMP

PROFILE
OF AN OLYMPIC GREAT

EDWIN MOSES

HE WON THE 1976 MONTREAL OLYMP-
ICS 400 METER HURDLES BY 8 METERS,
THE LARGEST WINNING MARGIN IN THE
HISTORY OF THE EVENT. THE U.S. BOY-
COTTED THE 1980 OLYMPICS BUT MOSES
RETURNED TO WIN THE EVENT IN THE
1984 OLYMPICS IN LOS ANGELES.

HE WON 107 STRAIGHT RACES OVER
A 9 YEAR PERIOD BEFORE BEING
DEFEATED.

HE WAS AN ENGINEERING AND PHY-
SICS STUDENT AT ATLANTA'S MOOR-
HOUSE COLLEGE WHICH HAD NO
TRACK AND FIELD PROGRAM.

HE RECEIVED AN ACADEMIC RATHER
THAN AN ATHLETIC SCHOLARSHIP.

THE SCHOOL HAD NO TRACK AND
FIELD PROGRAM SO HE HAD TO
WORK OUT AND TRAIN HIMSELF.

MEMORABLE TRACK AND FIELD MOMENT

MAY 25,
1935
at
ANN ARBOR
MICHIGAN

Jesse Owens

IN A BIG 10 CHAMPIONSHIP TRACK MEET HE JUMPED
26 FT. 8¼ INCHES, A WORLD RECORD, SPRINTED
100 YARDS IN 9.4 SECONDS, TYING HIS OWN WOR-
LD RECORD. HE RAN THE 220 YARD DASH IN 20.3
ANOTHER WORLD RECORD, WON THE 220 YARD
LOW HURDLES IN 22.6 SECONDS FOR YET ANO-
THER WORLD RECORD ALL COMPLETED IN THE
SAME DAY LESS THAN AN HOUR APART.

THE NIGHT BEFORE HE WAS SO SICK WITH THE FLU
NO ONE BELIEVED HE WOULD COMPETE AT ALL.

DR. LE ROY T. WALKER

WAS THE FIRST BLACK
PRESIDENT OF THE
UNITED STATES OLYMPIC
COMMITTEE.

BLACK ★Stars QUIZ

FROM OTHER LANDS

PICTURED BELOW ARE BLACK OLYMPIC STARS AND THEIR ACCOMPLI-
SHMENTS. CAN YOU GUESS FROM WHICH COUNTRY THEY ARE FROM.

1.)

DONOVAN BAILEY

HE WON THE 1996 OLYMPIC GAMES 100 METER DASH AT AT LOS ANGELES IN RECORD TIME. HE REPRESENTED

A.) TRINIDAD

B.) CANADA

C.) JAMAICA

2.)

FATUMA ROBA

IN THE 1996 OLYMPIC GAMES IN LOS ANGELES SHE BECAME THE FIRST WOMAN FROM HER PART OF THE WORLD TO WIN THE MARATHON.

A.) ETHIOPA

B.) ENGLAND

C.) SOUTH AFRICA

3.)

MARIE-JOSE PEREC

SHE WINS BOTH THE 200 AND 400 METER RACES AT THE 1996 OLYMPICS AT LOS ANGELES.

A.) FRANCE

B.) ETHIOPA

C.) TRINIDAD

NATION MATCH QUIZ

LISTED ON THE LEFT ARE OUTSTANDING BLACK ATHLETES FROM OTHER NATIONS. CAN YOU MATCH THE NAME WITH THEIR COUNTRY ON THE RIGHT. PLACE THE CORRECT LETTER IN THE SPACE PROVIDED.

1) GEORGE RHODEN · 400 METERS ___
2) LINFORD CHRISTIE · SPRINTER ___
3) BEN JOHNSON · SPRINTER ___
4) LLOYD LA BEACH · SPRINTER ___
5) MOSES KIPTANUI · DISTANCE RUNNER ___
6) ALBERTO JUANTORENA MID DISTANCE ___
7) ABEBE BIKILA · MARATHON ___

A. PANAMA
B. KENYA
C. JAMAICA
D. CANADA
E. CUBA
F. ETHIOPIA
G. ENGLAND

James Kwambai
A runner from Kenya specializing in the marathons. He won the Brescia and Beijing marathons, his first two marathons

Fatuma Roba
1996 she became the first Ethiopian women to win the Olympic gold medal in the marathon. A huge parade winding through the streets of Addis Ababa upon her return, cheered by thousands. She later won the Women's Boston Marathon

Evan Rutto
A Kenyan runner made the fastest ever debut marathon by winning the 2003 Chicago Marathon in a time of 2:05:50. He won the London Marathon and a second title in Chicago the following year

Mary Jepkosgei Ketany
The world's half-marathon champion from Kenya. Her personal best of 1:05:50 in the half marathon is the current women's world record.

Paul Kibil Tergat
A marathon runner from Brazil, one of the most influential marathon runners in the world. He currently holds the world record for the marathon, making his world record in Berlin in 2003, at 2:09:55. He is best known for winning the Saint Silvester Marathon Race five times after Nelson Mandella. He is the most celebrated African personality in Brazil.

Long Distance Runners III

Geoffrey Mutai
A Kenyan Long Distance runner who ran the fastest marathon ever, 2:03:02 at the 2011 Boston Marathon. The time will not be recognized by the international Accoation of Athletic Federation since the Boston curse does not meet the criteria to be eligible

Abebe Bikila
A two-time (1960 and 64) Olympic marathon champion the stadium in Addis Ababa, Ethiopia has been named after him,

Duncan Kibet
From Kenya, he became the second fastest marathoner ever when he won the Rotterdam Marathon with a time of 2:09:27.

Derartu Tulu
Ethiopian distance runner rose to fame and Olympic history when she convincingly won the women's 10,000 meters race at the Barcelona Olympics in 1992. The first gold medal win ever by an African woman.

Catherin Ndereba
She has twice won the marathon at the Worlds Championships and won silver in the 2004 and 2008. She is a four time winner of the Boston Marathon; she broke the women's marathon world record in 2001, running 2:18:17 at the Chicago Marathon. She was awarded the 20004 and 2005 Kenyan Sportswomen of the Year award

Long Distance Runners

What country do they represent?
Circle the correct answer

1) Haile Gebrselassie
He won two Olympic gold
medals over 10,00 meters
A) Ethiopia
B) Kenya
C) Somalia

2) Moses Kiptanui
The first to run the 3000 meter steeple
chase under 8 min.
A) Kenya
B) Egypt

4) Kipchoge Keino
Two-time Olympic gold
medalist 1500 meters and 3000
meters steeplechase (1968-1972)
A) France
B) Australia
C) Kenya

3) Meseret Defar
5000 meter Olympic Gold medal
winner (2008) broke world record in
even in 2006, again in 2008
A) Kenya
B) Ethiopia
C) Spain

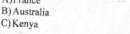

6) Mohammed Farah
Somalia born who hold British
Road record for 10,000
A) Brittan
B) Ethiopia
C) Egypt

5) Bernard Barmasa
Former Steeple chase world record
holder
A) Ethiopia
B) Kenya
C) South Africa

WOMEN TRACK and FIELD Icons

THE TENNESSEE STATE UNIVERSITY TIGER-BELLES 400 METER RELAY TEAM WHICH INCLUDED LEFT TO RIGHT: WILMA RUDOLPH, LUCIND WILLIAMS, BARBARA JONES AND MARTHA HUDSON WON THE EVENT IN THE ROME OLYMPICS HANDILY IN WORLD RECORD TIME OF 44 SECONDS.

REGINA JACOBS

AN OAKLAND (CA.) RESIDENT AND STANFORD GRADUATE SHE QUALIFIED FOR FOUR OLYMPICS AND COMPETED IN THREE (1988, '92 & '96) IN THE 1500 METER/MILE.

ANITA DE FRANTZ

IS THE FIRST AMERICAN WOMAN AND THE FIRST BLACK AMERICAN TO SIT ON THE INTERNATIONAL OLYMPIC COMMITTEE.

FLORENCE GRIFFITH JOYNER

AFFECTIONATELY KNOW AS "FLO JO", WON 4 MEDALS AT THE 1988 OLYMPICS IN SEOUL, BECOMING THE FIRST WOMAN TO WIN 4 MEDALS IN TRACK AND FIELD IN A SINGLE OLYMPICS. SHE WON GOLD IN THE 100 AND 200 METERS AND THE 400 METER RELAY, AND SILVER IN THE 1600 METER RELAY.

WYOMIA TYUS (BORN IN GEORGIA) ATTENDED TENNESSEE STATE UNIVERSITY. SHE WON THE OLYMPIC 100 METER DASH IN TOKYO IN A STUNNING, RECORD-SETTING 11.4 SECONDS.

FOUR YEARS LATER AT THE OLYMPIC GAMES IN MEXICO CITY, SHE BETTERED HER PREVIOUS RECORD AND RAN THE 100-METER DASH IN 11 SECONDS FLAT.

GOOD OLYMPIC STORIES ARE A TENSION RELIEVER!

SOUL CIRCLE

WYOMIA TYUS

Jackie Joyner-Kersee

SHE WAS THE FIRST U.S. WOMAN TO WIN THE OLYMPIC LONG JUMP AND THE FIRST ATHLETE IN 64 YEARS TO WIN BOTH A MULTI-EVENT COMPETITION AND AN INDIVIDUAL EVENT IN ONE OLYMPICS. SHE WON A SILVER MEDAL FOR THE HEPTATHLON AT THE 1984 OLYMPICS AND A GOLD MEDAL IN 1988 FOR THE HEPTATHLON, SETTING AN OLYMPIC AND WORLD RECORD. IN 1988 SHE AGAIN WON THE GOLD MEDAL FOR THE LONG JUMP AND SET AN OLYMPIC RECORD. WAS THE 1ST TO REPEAT AS HEPTATHLON CHAMPION (1992). BORN IN E. ST. LOUIS, A UCLA GRADUATE SHE WAS THE 1ST WOMAN TO RECEIVE THE SPORTING NEWS WATERFORD TROPHY.

WOMEN
IN THE OLYMPICS
SCRAMBLE Quiz

CAN YOU UNSCRAMBLE THE LAST NAMES OF THESE OLYMPIC WOMEN ATHLETES. THE INFORMATION UNDER THE PICTURE SHOULD AID YOU.

1.

WILMA PURODLH

SHE WAS THE FIRST WOMAN FROM THE U.S. TO WIN THREE GOLD MEDALS IN THE SAME OLYMPICS IN ROME (1960). SHE ATTENDED TENNESSEE STATE UNIVERSITY.

2.

MARION EOSJN

SHE WON THREE GOLD MEDALS AND TWO BRONZE MEDALS AT THE 2000 SUMMER OLYMPICS IN SYDNEY, AUSTRALIA TO BECOME THE MOST DECORATED FEMALE TRACK AND FIELD ATHLETE AT A SINGLE OLYMPIC GAME.

* SEE BELOW

3.

WILLYE HITWE

A MEMBER OF 5 U.S. OLYMPIC TEAMS (1956, 1960, 1964, 1968 AND 1972) WON A SILVER MEDAL AT MELBOURNE, AUSTRALIA IN THE LONG JUMP IN 1956, ANOTHER SILVER AT TOKYO AS A MEMBER OF THE 4×100 METER RELAY.

* SHE HAD TO RETURN ALL HER MEDALS AND SERVED JAIL TIME DUE TO STEROIDS

Other Sports

famous BLACK FIRSTS IN Golf

JOHN SHIPPEN JR.
1879-1968

IS THE FIRST AFRICAN-AMERICAN TO PLAY IN THE U.S. OPEN. BORN IN LONG ISLAND, N.Y. HE MOVED TO THE SHINNECOCK INDIAN RESERVATION WITH HIS FAMILY. HIS FATHER WAS A PASTOR ON THE RESERVATION.

THE OWNER OF THE GOLF COURSE BUILT THERE TAUGHT HIM TO PLAY. HE BECAME AN ACCOMPLISHED GOLFER AND FINE CADDY.

AT THE AGE OF 16 HE WAS SO TALENTED THAT HE WAS ENCOURAGED TO ENTER THE 1896 U.S. OPEN. HE TALKED HIS FRIEND OSCAR BUNN, A FULL BLOODED SHINNECOCK INDIAN INTO PLAYING ALSO.

SEVERAL OF THE ENGLISH AND SCOTTISH PROS PROTESTED THEIR PRESENCE THREATENING TO WITHDRAW. THEY PLAYED WHEN TOLD THE TOURNAMENT WOULD PLAY WITHOUT THEM.

HE SERVED AS GOLF PRO AT SEVERAL CLUBS UNTIL HE RETIRED IN 1960.

GOLF/SCRAMBLE

CAN YOU UNSCRAMBLE THE LAST NAMES OF THE NOTED GOLFERS. USE THE INFORMATION UNDER THE PICTURE TO AID YOU.

1.)

CALVIN ETEPE

HE WON THE 12TH ANNUAL TOURNAMENT PLAYERS CHAMPIONSHIP WINNING THE LARGEST PURSE (AT THE TIME) IN PGA HISTORY. IT WAS THE 10TH VICTORY IN HIS PRO CAREER.

2.)

LEE LERED

HE'S THE FIRST AFRICAN AMERICAN TO COMPETE AGAINST WHITES IN S. AFRICA. IN 1974 HE BECAME THE FIRST BLACK TO QUALIFY FOR THE MASTERS TOURNAMENT.

3.)

CHARLIE FOSIRFD

HE WAS THE FIRST AFRICAN-AMERICAN TO WIN A P.G.A. EVENT, THE 1967 HARTFORD OPEN. HE LEARNED THE GAME AS A YOUNG BOY CADDYING AT THE ALL WHITE CAROLINAS COUNTRY CLUB IN CHARLOTTE, N. CAROLINA.

THAT TIGER WOODS IS A B·A·A·D BROTHER

HE WON 25 PER CENT OF HIS PRO TOURNAMENTS

ONE WIN IN FOUR IS FABULOUS

AND HE ONLY PLAYS IN ABOUT HALF OF THE SCHEDULED TOURNAMENTS

MORRE

TIGER'S A LEGEND IN HIS SPARE TIME!

Tiger Woods

PRO FILES

HE WAS THE YOUNGEST GOLFER TO WIN ALL 4 MAJOR GOLF CHAMPIONSHIPS (THE MASTERS, PGA, THE U.S. OPEN, AND THE BRITISH OPEN).

HE HAD A SPECTACULAR AMATEUR CAREER THAT BEGAN AT AGE 3.

HE WAS THE FIRST BLACK AND THE YOUNGEST PLAYER PLAYER TO WIN THE U.S. JUNIOR AMATEUR GOLFING TITLE.

HE MADE A HOLE IN ONE WHILE STILL A GRADE SCHOOL GOLFER.

THAT TIGER WOODS REALLY KNOWS HIS WAY AROUND A GOLF COURSE

SPORTS

WHAT DO YOU THINK HIS SECRET IS, RALPH?

MORRE

THE HOLES ARE NUMBERED, SYBIL

famous BLACK firsts in HOCKEY

WILLIE O'REE

HOW COME AFRICAN-AMERICANS NEVER PLAY HOCKEY, RANDY?

YOU NEVER HEARD OF WILLIE O'REE, CONNIE?

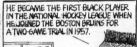

HE BECAME THE FIRST BLACK PLAYER IN THE NATIONAL HOCKEY LEAGUE WHEN HE JOINED THE BOSTON BRUINS FOR A TWO-GAME TRIAL IN 1957.

IN THE 60-61 SEASON, HE PLAYED 43 GAMES, MAKING 4 GOALS AND 10 ASSISTS.

SOUL CIRCLE

1935
WILLIE O'REE

Hockey Scramble Quiz

CAN YOU UNSCRAMBLE THE NAMES OF THESE BLACK PRO HOCKEY PLAYERS?
USE THE CLUES UNDER THE PICTURES

1.)

GRANT
HURF
HE WAS GOAL TENDER FOR THE EDMONTON OILERS. HE ASSISTED ON WAYNE GRETZKY'S RECORD 50 GOALS IN 39 GAMES.

2.)

TONY
Mc GEKYEN
HE WAS THE FIRST BLACK PLAYER ON THE BUFFALO SABRES OF THE NHL.

3.)

RAY
NEDFLUE
HE WAS ONE OF ONLY FOUR BLACK HOCKEY STARS PLAYING IN THE NATIONAL HOCKEY LEAGUE IN THE 1984-85 SEASON.

ARTHUR DORRINGTON
WAS THE FIRST BLACK PLAYER TO PLAY IN ORGANIZED HOCKEY. HE PLAYED 1950-51 SEASON WITH JOHNSTOWN (PA.) JETS.

4.)

ALTON
TIHEW
HE WAS THE SECOND BLACK HOCKEY PLAYER TO PERFORM FOR AN AMERICAN LEAGUE HOCKEY TEAM (N.Y. RAIDERS).

I WANT TO BE THE YOUNGEST JOCKEY

DO YOU KNOW ABOUT ALONZO "LONNIE" CLAYTON?

HE SHARES THE RECORD AS THE YOUNGEST KENTUCKY DERBY WINNER, HAVING RIDDEN TO VICTORY ON "AZRA" AT AGE 15 IN 1892.

I WANNA BE A DISC JOCKEY!

SOUL CIRCLE

8-10

ALONZO (LONNIE) CLAYTON

FAMOUS BLACK FIRSTS in HORSE RACING

ISAAC MURPHY
1856-1896

HE WAS THE FIRST JOCKEY TO WIN THE KENTUCKY DERBY THREE TIMES AND THE FIRST TO WIN TWO CONSECUTIVE YEARS.

HE WAS A WINNING JOCKEY AT OTHER RACING VENUES SUCH AS SARATOGA WHERE HE WON 49 OUT OF 51 RACES.

HIS CAREER RECORD WAS 628 WINS OUT OF 1,412 STARTS.

IN 1884 HE WON HIS FIRST KENTUCKY DERBY RIDING "BUCHANAN" WHICH WAS OWNED BY WILLIAM BIRD, AN AFRICAN-AMERICAN.

JOCKEY OLIVER LEWIS HOLDS THE RECORD AS THE FIRST WINNER OF THE KENTUCKY DERBY IN 1875

HE LATER BECAME A TRAINER

OLIVER LEWIS

WILLIAM WALKER WAS ONCE CONSIDERED AMERICA'S TOP JOCKEY, NIPPER! HIS WIN IN THE KENTUCKY DERBY IN 1877...

WAS THE FIRST FOR AN AFRICAN-AMERICAN RIDER AND TRAINER

HOW ABOUT THAT! A WALKER WHO RIDES

SOUL CIRCLE

1-25

WILLIAM WALKER

FAMOUS BLACK FIRSTS in TENNIS

ARTHUR ASHE (1943-'93)

IN 1975 HE BECAME THE FIRST AFRICAN-AMERICAN MALE TO WIN THE WIMBLEDON TENNIS SINGES TITLE.

HE DIED AS A RESULT OF AIDS-RELATED PNEUMONIA, DUE TO A TAINTED BLOOD TRANSFUSION.

ORA WASHINGTON (1898-1971) WAS THE 1ST BLACK WOMAN TO WIN 7 CONSECUTIVE TITLES IN THE AMERICAN TENNIS ASSOCIATION.

SHE BEGAN HER CAREER IN 1924.

TENNIS QUIZ

CAN YOU CHECK THE CORRECT ANSWER FROM THE 3 FACTS LISTED UNDER THE PICTURE OF THE TENNIS STAR BELOW.

ALTHEA GIBSON

SHE WON THE WOMEN'S SINGLE TENNIS CHAMPIONSHIP AT WIMBLEDON, ENGLAND IN 1957 AND '58 BECOMING THE FIRST AFRICAN-AMERICAN TO WIN THE TITLE. SHE BECAME A STAR IN WHAT OTHER SPORT?

A.) PING PONG
B.) BASKETBALL
C.) GOLF

1948 REGINALD WEIR

A PHYSICIAN OF N.Y. CITY WAS THE FIRST BLACK TO PARTICIPATE IN THE U.S. INDOOR LAWN TENNIS ASSOCIATION CHAMPIONSHIP IN NEW YORK CITY.

VENUS

SERENA

THE WILLIAMS SISTERS TOGETHER WON THE WOMEN'S DOUBLES TITLE AT WIMBLEDON. WHICH SISTER WON THE WIMBLEDON WOMEN'S SINGLE CHAMPIONSHIP?

A.) VENUS
B.) SERENA
C.) BOTH

TENNIS HISTORY

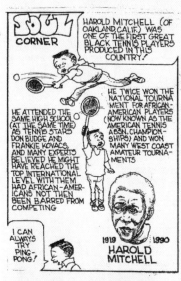

SOUL CORNER

HAROLD MITCHELL (OF OAKLAND, CALIF.) WAS ONE OF THE FIRST GREAT BLACK TENNIS PLAYERS PRODUCED IN THIS COUNTRY!

HE ATTENDED THE SAME HIGH SCHOOL (AT THE SAME TIME) AS TENNIS STARS DON BUDGE AND FRANKIE KOVACS AND MANY EXPERTS BELIEVED HE MIGHT HAVE REACHED THE TOP INTERNATIONAL LEVEL WITH THEM HAD AFRICAN-AMERICANS NOT THEN BEEN BARRED FROM COMPETING

HE TWICE WON THE NATIONAL TOURNAMENT FOR AFRICAN-AMERICAN PLAYERS (NOW KNOWN AS THE AMERICAN TENNIS ASSN. CHAMPIONSHIPS) AND WON MANY WEST COAST AMATEUR TOURNAMENTS

I CAN ALWAYS TRY PING-PONG!

1918   1990
HAROLD MITCHELL

THE FIRST BLACK NATIONAL TENNIS TOURNAMENT

THE FIRST BLACK NATIONAL TENNIS TOURNAMENT WAS HELD IN BALTIMORE, MARYLAND AT DRUID HILL PARK IN 1917.
THE FIRST BLACK NATIONAL CHAMPION WAS TALLEY HOMES WHO WON IN 1918, 1921 AND 1924.

ORA WASHINGTON OF THE PHILADELPHIA YWCA WAS A REMARKABLE WOMAN TENNIS PLAYER. SHE WAS UNDEFEATED FOR 12 YEARS.

SHE WON 201 TROPHIES AND 8 TITLES IN 9 YEARS.

TENNIS LEGEND

Reginald Weir

HE WAS CAPTAIN OF THE CITY COLLEGE OF NEW YORK'S TENNIS TEAM. HE WAS SINGLES CHAMPION 1931, 1932, 1933, 1937, AND 1942.

HE SOUGHT ENTRY INTO THE UNITED STATES LAWN TENNIS ASSOCIATION IN 1927 AND WAS REJECTED BY THE EXECUTIVE COMMITTEE.

HE HAD TO WAIT UNTIL 1948, A 20 YEAR WAIT, BEFORE HE WAS ALLOWED TO COMPETE IN A USLTA TOURNAMENT, WHICH WAS WELL PAST HIS PRIME.

ZINA GARRISON

SHE BECAME THE FIRST AFRICAN-AMERICAN OLYMPIC MEDAL WINNER IN TENNIS (1988) WHEN SHE WON GOLD IN DOUBLES AND BRONZE IN SINGLES.

OTHER STARS AND CHAMPIONS

CISERO MURPHY
1937-1996

KNOWN AS THE "BROOKLYN KID" CHAMPION BILLIARDS PLAYER DURING THE 50'S AND 60'S BREAKING DOWN RACIAL BARRIERS IN THE SPORT.

NIKKI FRANKE

U.S. FENCING ASSOCIATION'S NATIONAL CHAMPION IN 1975 AND 1980. HER GREATEST CONTRIBUTION TO HER HAS BEEN AS A COACH.

HARRY EDWARDS

A FORMER SAN JOSE STATE ATHLETE LEADING ACADEMIC SPOKESMAN FOR FOR THE EFFECT OF SPORTS ON SOCIETY ESPECIALLY AS IT RELATES TO RACE AND CULTURE.

SHANI DAVIS

HE BECAME THE FIRST BLACK MAN TO WIN WINTER OLYMPICS GOLD MEDAL (IN SPEED SKATING IN 2006 OLYMPICS)

GIRLS CAN'T PLAY PRO BASEBALL, SYBIL

YOU'VE NEVER HEARD OF *TONI STONE*, RALPH?

IN 1953, SHE APPEARED IN ABOUT 50 GAMES FOR THE INDIANAPOLIS CLOWNS, A NEGRO LEAGUE FRANCHISE. SHE PLAYED SECOND BASE AND BATTED .243. SHE MAY HAVE BEEN THE ONLY FEMALE PLAYER IN THE NEGRO LEAGUES.

4-13

I SUPPOSE HER LAST NAME WAS LIKE HER HANDS.

SOUL CIRCLE

1921

TONI STONE

People are talking about....

Stephanie Hightower
Track&Field president and chairman of the board of US ATF

Monta Ellis
Golden State Warriors high scoring guard

Sanya Richards
She broke the U.S. Record in the 400 meters at 48.70 in 2006, and was named IAAF Female World Athlete of the Year.

David Shaw
Stanford Univ. Football Coach

Roy Jones JR.
He is the only boxer in history to start as a Jr. Middleweight and go on to win a heavyweight title. He is also a record seven Belts at the same time

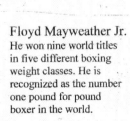

Floyd Mayweather Jr.
He won nine world titles in five different boxing weight classes. He is recognized as the number one pound for pound boxer in the world.

Dr. Evie Dennis
A leader in Track and Field for Four decades

Headliners

WHO AM I?

I'm from Pomona, CA I was born in 1971. I have won world title in three boxing division, an I'm the former WBA Welter Weight Super-Champion. As an am amateur. MY record was 96-3.

A. Floyd Mayweather Jr.
B. Shame Mosley
C. Roy Jones Jr.

Hue Jackson
He became head football coach of the Oakland Raiders after serving the team as offensive coordinator.

Tyson Gay
He ran a 9.69 second 100 meter dash which was an American Record the second fastest time ever recorded.

Justin Gatlin

Brooklyn, N.Y. native came to Univ., of Tenn. As a hurdler. Became a sprinter, winning gold medal in the 100 Meter Dash at 2004 Summer Olympics.

83

Shelly Ann Fraser
Jamaican sprinter who was first Jamaican woman in history to win an Olympic gold medal in the 100

(In Record Time)

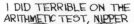

Historical
SPORTS FIGURES

BILL RICHMOND
"THE BLACK TERROR"

BORN IN STATEN ISLAND, N.Y. IN 1777. HE WAS DISCOVERED WHEN THE BRITISH OCCUPIED NEW YORK. GENERAL PERCY, A COMMANDER OF THE BRITISH TROOPS TOOK HIM BACK TO ENGLAND WHERE HE BECAME A FAMOUS FIGHTER, WINNING ONE BOUT AT THE AGE OF 56.

JOHN BORICAN

DISTANCE RUNNER OF THE 30'S FROM VIRGINIA STATE COLLEGE WHO TWICE DEFEATED THE ERA'S GREATEST MILER, GLEN CUNNINGHAM.

SAM McVEY

A GREAT HEAVYWEIGHT FIGHTER OF THE 1900'S WHO FOUGHT THE GREAT JACK JOHNSON 3 TIMES.

HARRY McDONALD

HARD RUNNING HALF BACK WHO PLAYED FOR ROCHESTER JEFFERSONS IN 1912.

WILLIAM "DOLLY" KING

FROM LONG ISLAND UNIVERSITY - PLAYED PRO BASKETBALL WITH THE ALL-BLACK DAYTON RENS IN 1948.

KID CHOCOLATE

BORN ELIGIO SARDINIAS IN CUBA IN 1910. HE WON THE JUNIOR LIGHTWEIGHT TITLE BY A K.O. OVER BENNIE BASS IN 1931 THEN TOOK THE FEATHERWEIGHT CHAMPIONSHIP FROM LEW FELDMAN IN 1932.

LUKE EASTER

SIGNED BY CLEVELAND IN 1948 AFTER LEADING BIRMINGHAM BLACK BARRONS TO NEGRO WORLD SERIES WIN.

Viewing Sports Stars

NATALIE RANDOLPH IS ONE OF THE NATION'S ONLY HIGH SCHOOL (COOLIDGE HIGH SCHOOL, WASHINGTON, D.C.) FOOTBALL COACHES.

SHE IS A SCIENCE TEACHER AND FORMER COLLEGE TRACK STAR, AND PRO WOMEN'S FOOTBALL PLAYER.

SHE GREW UP AND ATTENDED SCHOOLS IN WASHINGTON, D.C. WHERE SHE PARTICIPATED IN VOLLEY BALL, BASKETBALL AND TRACK.

SHE WENT ON TO THE UNIV. OF VIRGINIA PARTLY ON A TRACK SCHOLARSHIP AND LEFT THERE WITH A BACHELOR DEGREE IN ENVIRONMENTAL SCIENCE AND A MASTERS IN EDUCATION.

SHE PLAYED WIDE RECEIVER FOR THE D.C. DIVAS OF THE INDEPENDENT WOMAN'S FOOTBALL LEAGUE FROM 2003 TO 2008. SHE BECAME A SCIENCE TEACHER IN A DISTRICT HIGH SCHOOL IN 2005.

NATALIE IS COMMITTED TO HELPING HER PLAYER SCORE ON THE FIELD.... AND IN LIFE.

SHE'S SMART ON THE FIELD AND OFF THE FIELD

Natalie Randolph

Pumpsie Green
In 1959 he became the Boston Red Sox first black player and the Red Sox became the Last Major League team to integrate.

Cam Newton
Auburn Quarterback when he won the Heisman-2010

Michael Vick
Philadelphia Eagles quarterback, one of the best in the National Football League

Mike Singletary
Legendary Chicago Bears linebacker is S.F. 49er first black Head Coach

87

Sports
HEADLINERS
OF THE RECENT PAST

WILLIE BROWN (60'S - 70'S)
(OAKLAND RAIDER CORNERBACK) ONE OF THE FINEST IN PRO FOOTBALL HISTORY. HE HELD A PRO RECORD 54 INTERCEPTIONS RANKING AMONG NFL ALL TIME LEADERS.

JIM HINES

A McCLYMONDS OF OAKLAND HIGH SCHOOL/TEXAS SOUTHERN UNIVERSITY SPRINTER WON THE 100 METER DASH AT THE 1968 OLYMPICS IN MEXICO IN A RECORD 9.9 SECONDS.

BARNEY EWELL
TOP SPRINTER OF THE MID 1940'S WITH PANAMANIAN LLYOD LA BEACH TOOK 2nd IN BOTH THE 100 AND 200 METERS AT LONDON 1948 OLYMPICS PLUS A GOLD IN THE 4 X 100 RELAY.

GEORGE FOSTER

HE BECAME THE NATIONAL LEAGUES M.V.P. IN 1977, WON 3 CONSECUTIVE R.B.I. TITLES, 1976 THRU 1978 WHILE PLAYING FOR THE CINCINNAI REDS.

ROD CAREW
HE WON 7 AMERICAN LEAGUE BATTING TITLES BEGINNING IN 1972 WITH MINNESOTA.

JIM RICE
POWER HITTING OUTFIELDER FOR THE BOSTON RED. HE WAS M.V.P. IN 1978.

FAMED RAIDER TIGHT-END OF THE 70'S WHO ALSO WAS A STAR FOR THE BALTIMORE COLTS.

RAYMOND CHESTER

Sepia Soul Circle

Dwight Phillips

He was a promising sprinter In his early days but concentrated on the triple jump while at Univ. of Kentucky before switching to the long jump after moving to Arizona State Univ. in 2000.

He came to prominence in 2003 when both indoor world championships.

He won a Gold Medal at the 2004 Athens Olympics.

Richard Seymour

The Raider's defensive tackle signed a new contract in 2011, making him the highest paid lineman in the NFL.

John Wall

Basketball player, College; Kentucky, chosen first Overall in the 2010 NBA Draft by the Washington Wizards.

He played his high school ball at Word of God Christian Academy in Raleigh, North Carolina.

WINNERS

Blake Griffin

Basketball forward for the L.A. Clippers who picked him number one in round in 2009. While still at the UNN, of Oklahoma Sooners, he was named NAISMITH player of the year, Oscar Robertson Trophy, John Wooden Award and the Adolf Rupp Trophy

George Crowe

He was at the forefront of breaking racial barriers in basketball and baseball in the 1940's.

He played basketball for the N.Y. Harlem Renaissance.

After being named "Mr. Basketball" (The best high school basketball player in the state)

He broke into baseball's Big League n 1952 with the Boston Braves at age 31.

Manute Bol

Sudanese-born basketball player and activist. At 7ft 7in he was the second tallest player to ever appear in the NBA. He was the first African born drafted into the NBA. He was also famous for his activism on behalf of his country.

LaShawn Merritt

He won the World Junior Championship in 2004, in the 400 Meter Dash.

He won the Olympic Gold Medal in the 400 Meter Dash in Beijing with a personal best 43.75.

He was a part of the 4x400 relay team that won the relay at the Beijing Olympic Games.

He was suspended for 21 months for failing a doping test.

Sugar Ray Robinson
(1920-1989)
Recorded 89 amateur fights with 69 knockouts in the first round winner and 1940 lightweight Golden Glove titles. He turned pro in 1940.

90

WHO what *WHEN* and where
Super Bowl XLI · Sunday Feb.4,'07 · Miami, Fla.

LOVIE SMITH

NATIONAL FOOTBALL LEAGUE HISTORY WAS MADE WHEN LOVIE SMITH (COACH OF THE CHICAGO BEARS) AND TONY DUNGY (COACH OF THE INDIANAPOLIS COLTS) BECAME THE FIRST AFRICAN-AMERICANS TO LEAD THEIR TEAMS TO THE SUPER BOWL.
(WON BY THE COLTS 29 TO 17)

PETER WESTBROOK

KNOWN AS AMERICA'S GREATEST FENCER OF THE 20TH CENTURY. HE IS A SIX-TIME OLYMPIAN AND MEDALIST.

DOMINIQUE DAWES

SHE HELPED THE USA WOMEN'S GYMNASTICS TEAM WIN THE 1996 OLYMPIC GYMNASTIC TITLE IN ATLANT, GA.

PROfile
national football league

VINCE YOUNG

HE LEAD HIS UNIVERSITY OF TEXAS LONGHORNS TO THE NATIONAL COLLEGIATE 2005 CHAMPIONSHIP.
HE WAS THE FIRST NATIONAL FOOTBALL LEAGUE DRAFT CHOICE BY THE TENNESSEE TITANS.
HE WON THE 2006 OFFENSIVE ROOKIE OF THE YEAR AWARD.

2007
MIKE TOMLIN

BECOMES THE FIRST AFRICAN-AMERICAN COACH OF THE PITTSBURGH STEELERS.

91

HUMOR IN HUE

"YOU'RE GOING TO BECOME A BASKETBALL STAR!"

"Wow!, Just think what he could do without the sign"

SPORTS POTPOURRI...

IRIS SMITH

BECAME THE FIRST BLACK WOMAN TO WIN A WRESTLING GOLD MEDAL. (159 LB. CLASS IN 2005).

ANNICE CANADY

WAS THE FIRST FEMALE COLLEGE FOOTBALL OFFICIAL IN DIVISION I-AA.

VIOLET PALMER

WAS THE FIRST AFRICAN-AMERICAN WOMAN HIRED TO REFEREE IN THE NBA.

ANITA L. DE FRANTZ

A MEMBER OF THE 1976 AND 1980 OLYMPIC ROWING TEAMS, SHE BECAME THE FIRST WOMAN AND THE FIRST BLACK AMERICAN TO SIT ON THE OLYMPIC COMMITTEE.

EFFA MANLEY

WAS THE FIRST WOMAN ELECTED TO THE NATIONAL BASEBALL HALL OF FAME (IN 2006). SHE WAS CO-OWNER, WITH HER HUSBAND, OF THE NEWARK EAGLES OF THE NEGRO LEAGUE.

BILL LESTER

AN OAKLAND (CAL.) NATIVE IN MARCH 2006 BECAME THE FIRST BLACK DRIVER TO COMPETE IN NASCAR'S TOP SERIES SINCE WILLY T. RIBBS IN 1986.

Quiz and Games

POTPOURRI
TRUE OR FALSE
QUIZ

FRANK
THOMAS

MIKE GARRETT

JASON KIDD

BILL SPILLER

BUCK O'NEIL

MAURY WILLS

DWIGHT
GOODEN

CHRIS
WEBBER

OZZIE
NEWSOME

NATE THURMOND

Potpourri
True or False Quiz

	True	False
1. Frank Thomas known for his menacing home run power was nicknamed "The Big Hurt"	☐	☐
2. Mike Garrett Eleusive running back for U.S.C. became the school's first black athlete director	☐	☐
3. Ozzie Newsome starred at tight-end for the Univ. of Alabama before being drafted by Cleveland. He was called "The Wizard of OZ"	☐	☐
4. Jason Kidd Played high school basketball in Hayward, CA. The Univ. of Cal, then pros.	☐	☐
5. Chris Webber played his college ball at Michigan before being drafted number one by Sacramento Kings	☐	☐
6. Maury Wills was best known for his dramatic home runs	☐	☐
7. Buck O'Neil gained his fame in Negro League Basketball	☐	☐
8. Bill Spiller was one of the pioneers in golf. The PGA granted hime postumous membership in 2010.	☐	☐
9. Dwight Gooden was a star pitcher for the Yankees	☐	☐
10. Nate Thurmond was a All-Star baketball center for the LA Lakers	☐	☐

Star Scramble Quiz

CAN YOU UNSCRAMBLE THE NAMES OF THESE STAR ATHLETES BY USING THE CLUES UNDER THE PICTURES.

① DEBBIE SATOHM

SHE WAS THE FIRST BLACK SKATER ON A WORLD TEAM SHE WON THE 1985 UNITED STATES AND WORLD FIGURE SKATING CHAMPIONSHIP.

② LEEP

AN ALL TIME SOCCER GREAT WHO LED BRAZIL TO WORLD SOCCER TITLES.

GEORGE BRANHAM III WAS THE FIRST AFRICAN-AMERICAN TO WIN THE FIRESTONE TOURNAMENT OF CHAMPIONS (1993). HE WON TWO CHAMPIONSHIPS IN LESS THAN A MONTH INCLUDING THE BALTIMORE OPEN.

soul corner

FREDDY ADU AT AGE 14, IS THE YOUNGEST PLAYER TO BE DRAFTED TO...

... A MAJOR LEAGUE TEAM MAKING HIM THE YOUNGEST PROFESSIONAL ATHLETE IN TEAM SPORTS.

HE HAS CONTRACTS WITH MLS, NIKE AND PEPSI. BORN IN GHANA HIS FAMILY MOVED TO POTOMAC, MD.

I'D BETTER STEP UP ON MY SOCCER PRACTICE

Freddy Adu

FLO HYMAN ALMOST SINGLE-HANDEDLY CHANGED THE WAY VOLLEYBALL IS PLAYED SHE LED THE U.S. TEAM TO A SILVER MEDAL IN THE 1984 OLYMPICS

SHE DIED SUDDENLY IN 1986 AT AGE 32 OF A RARE HEART DISORDER

SHE DESERVES A SUPER-SOUL SISTER SALUTE!

12-21

SOUL CIRCLE

FLO HYMAN

ATHLETES PUZZLE

CAN YOU COMPLETE THE LAST NAME OF THE ATHLETES PICTURED ON THIS PAGE ON THE PUZZLE BELOW

6. BILLY
LEADER OF NBA
PLAYER'S UNION

2. DAVID
BOSTON
RED SOX
HOME RUN
HITTER

1. HAKEEM
7-FOOTER FROM
NIGERIA WHO
BECAME PART OF
HOUSTON ROCKETS
"TWIN TOWERS"

3. OZZIE
TOP DEFENSIVE
SHORTSTOP
OF HIS DECADE

8. DAVID "THE ADMIRAL"
NAVAL ACADEMY GRAD.
PLAYED ON NBA CHAMP-
ION SAN ANTONIO SPURS

7. DWYANE
HOT SHOOTING
MIAMI HEAT
NBA '05-'06
CHAMPIONS

5. GENE
HE PLAYED 2ND BASE
FOR CHICAGO CUBS
TO ERNIE BANKS
SHORTSTOP

4. LADAINIAN
SAN DIEGO'S MVP
RUNNING BACK

96

COACHES CORNER

LISTED AT TOP OF THIS PAGE ARE NAMES OF COACHES/MANAGERS OF ATHLETIC TEAMS. LISTED AT THE BOTTOM ARE TEAMS THEY MANAGED OR COACHED. CAN YOU MATCH THE NAME AT THE TOP WITH HIS TEAM AT THE BOTTOM. INSERT CORRECT LETTER IN SPACE PROVIDED.

COACHES/MANAGERS

ROMEO CRENNEL

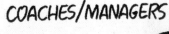

1 LENNY WILKENS _____
2 DUSTY BAKER _____
3 FELIPE ALOU _____
4 TONY DUNGY _____
5 CITO GASTON _____
6 K.C. JONES _____
7 TYRONE WILLINGHAM __
8 ROMEO CRENEL _____
9 TONY PEREZ _____
10 ART SHELL _____
11 LOVIE SMITH _____
12 AVERY JOHNSON _____

FELIPE ALOU

CITO GASTON

LENNY WILKENS

TONY DUNGY

TEAMS

A CLEVELAND BROWNS
B NOTRE DAME
C CAPITOL BULLETS
D OAKLAND RAIDERS
E CINCINNATI REDS
F SEATTLE SUPERSONICS
G INDIANOPOLIS COLTS
H TORONTO BLUE JAYS
I MONTREAL EXPOS
J CHICAGO CUBS
K CHICAGO BEARS
L DALLAS MAVERICKS

TYRONE WILLINGHAM

K.C. JONES

DUSTY BAKER

Sports Quiz

CAN YOU GUESS THE CORRECT ANSWERS TO THE QUESTIONS BELOW CIRCLE THE CORRECT ANSWER

1.
WENDELL OLIVER SCOTT

WAS THE FIRST BLACK AUTO RACE CAR DRIVER TO:

A.) QUALIFY FOR THE INDY 500 RACE

B.) WIN A NASTAR (WINSTON CUP

C.) SUSPENDED FOR DRIVING VIOLATIONS

2.
WILLY RIBBS

WHO BEGAN RACING IN SAN JOSE, CA. WAS THE FIRST BLACK RACE DRIVER TO:

A.) WIN A NASTAR WINSTON CUP

B.) CRASH AT THE INDY SPEEDWAY

C.) QUALIFY FOR THE INDY 500 RACE

WHO AM I?
BICYCLE RACER

I BEGAN MY CAREER BY WORKING AT A BICYCLE SHOP IN INDIANA. I GOT INTO MY FIRST REAL CONTEST AT THE AGE OF 13 WHEN MY EMPLOYER ENTERED ME INTO A RACE TO AMUSE THE SPECTATORS. I WON HANDILY AND I CONTINUED TO WIN, DESPITE THE RESENTMENT OF MY OPPONENT IN RACES THROUGHOUT AMERICA AS WELL AS ENGLAND AND AUSTRALIA

A.) JOE LASHLEY

B.) WILLIAM RHODMAN

C.) MAJOR TAYLOR

3.

CHERYL DANIELS

DURING HER 24 YEAR PROFESSIONAL BOWLING CAREER SHE HAS AMASSED NUMEROUS TITLES, BEING TWICE VOTED PRO WOMENS ASSOCIATION PLAYER OF THE YEAR. SHE HAILS FROM: (A.) DETROIT, MICH. B.) BERKELEY, CA. C.) LOUISVILLE, KY.

DIANE DURHAM

IN 1981 SHE BECAME THE FIRST AFRICAN-AMERICAN WOMAN TO WIN THE UNITED STATES GYMNASTICS CHAMPIONSHIPS FOR TWO CONSECUTIVE YEARS.

name the athlete quiz

CAN YOU NAME THE ATHLETES PICTURED BELOW. FIND BY READING THE CLUES UNDER THE PICTURE

1.)

LYNETTE
`W` ` ` ` ` ` ` `

ALL TIME LEADING SCORER IN WOMAN'S BASKETBALL SCORER AND TOP SCORER AT UNIV. OF KANSAS.
SHE WAS THE FIRST WOMAN TO PLAY FOR THE HARLEM GLOBETROTTERS IN 1985.
SHE STARRED ON THE GOLD MEDAL-WINNING U.S. OLYMPIC BASKETBALL TEAM.

2.)

ALTHEA
`G` ` ` ` ` ` ` `

SHE WAS THE FIRST AFRICAN-AMERICAN TO WIN THE WIMBLEDON TENNIS TITLE WINNING 1957 AND 1958.
SHE WENT ON TO BECOME A WOMEN'S GOLF CHAMPION.
SHE WAS INDUCTED INTO THE INTERNATIONAL TENNIS HALL OF FAME IN 1971.

3.)

SHERYL
`S` ` ` ` ` ` ` `

HOUSTON COMETS WOMEN'S BASKETBALL STAR, 5 TIMES ALL STAR, 3 TIMES OLYMPIC GOLD MEDALIST, WBNA CHAMPION AS MEMBER OF COMETS.
AS A COLLEGIATE PLAYER SHE BROUGHT TEXAS TECH A NATIONAL CHAMPIONSHIP SCORING 47 POINTS IN THE FINAL GAME OF 1993.

JIMMY CLAXTON PITCHED FOR THE OAKLAND OAKS OF THE PACIFIC COAST LEAGUE IN A GAME AGAINST THE VISITING LOS ANGELES ANGELS ON MAY 20, 1916

30 YEARS BEFORE JACKIE ROBINSON BROKE BASEBALL'S COLOR LINE – IN THE YEARS BEFORE WWI. HE WAS A PITCHER WITH THE ALL BLACK OAKLAND GIANTS

HE WAS INTRODUCED TO THE OAKS BY A NATIVE-AMERICAN WHO PRESENTED HIM AS A "FELLOW TRIBESMAN"

SOUL CIRCLE

JIMMY CLAXTON.

JERSEY NUMBER QUIZ

CAN YOU MATCH THE ATHLETE ON THE LEFT WITH THE JERSEY NUMBER HE MADE FAMOUS ON THE RIGHT. ENTER NUMBER IN SPACE PROVIDED.

A. EMMITT SMITH _____
FOOTBALL

B. HENRY AARON _____
BASEBALL

C. JIM BROWN _____
FOOTBALL

D. KOBE BRYANT _____
BASKETBALL

E. WALTER PAYTON _____
FOOTBALL

F. JACKIE ROBINSON _____
BASEBALL

G. JERRY RICE _____
FOOTBALL

H. WILLIE MAYS _____
BASEBALL

I. BARRY SANDERS _____
FOOTBALL

J. MICHAEL JORDAN _____
BASKETBALL

42 32 34 8 22 80 23 24 44 20

JERRY RICE OF THE SAN FRANCISCO 49ers HAS CAUGHT A RECORD-SETTING 1000 PASSES, MAKING HIM THE GREATEST PASS-CATCHER THAT EVER LIVED...

HE'S REALLY GOT IT, JERRY

GOT WHAT, NIPPER?

THE GIFT OF GRAB!

Media Quiz

Can you select the correct answer to the questions about these sports stars below? Circle the right answer

①

Lennox Lewis

Retired British boxer and undisputed world heavyweight championship. Won 1988 Olympic Games after defeating future world heavyweight champ:

A. Time Witherspoon
B. Riddick Bowe
C. Michael Spinks

②

Chris Paul

New Orleans Hornets pro basketball guard, born and raised in North Carolina was Rookie of the Year, 2006. He is known for another sport

A. Bowling
B. Golf
C. Tennis

③

Kenenisa Bekele

Ethiopia Long-Distance who holds two World Records and Olympic Records in what Events?

A. 1500 & 5000
B. 1500 & 10,000
C. 5000 & 10,000

④

Ray Allen

Boston Celtics Shooting Guard and Collegiately for Univ. of Connecticut. Recently became number one three-point scorer in the NBA. Former 3 point top score was:

A. Reggie Miller
B. Kobe Bryant
C. LeBron James

⑤

Asafa Powell

Jamaican sprinter who held the World Record in the 100 Meters between June 05 and May 08 with times of 9.77 and 9.74 he has:

A. Broken the 10 sec barrier in the 100 M more then any one else
B. Has completed more Olympic Games than any other sprinter
C. Has represented more countries in the Olympic Game than anyone else

TRUE OR FALSE - (mark T or F)

1 WOMAN BASKETBALLER LISA LESLIE WAS A 4 TIME OLYMPIC GOLD MEDAL WINNER ___

2 TENNIS STAR VENUS WILLIAMS HAS 7 GRAND SLAM SINGLES TITLES ___

3 BASEBALLER MIGUEL TEJADA'S NICKNAME IS "LA GUA GUA" WHICH MEANS "THE BUS" IN CERTAIN SPANISH DIALECTS. ___

4 DERREK LEE WAS THE 2005 NATIONAL LEAGUE BATTING CHAMPION ___

5 PRINCE FIELDER IS THE SON OF ENTERTAINER PRINCE ___

6 LA SHAWN MERRITT WAS BANNED FOR 2 YEARS FOR USING A MALE ENHANCEMENT DRUG AFTER WINNING THE 800 METERS IN THE 2008 OLYMPICS. ___

7 BOSTON CELTICS PAUL PIERCE IS KNOWN AS "THE TRUTH" ___

8 CARMELO ANTHONY LED GEORGETOWN TO THE 2003 NATIONAL BASKETBALL CHAMPIONSHIP ___

9 WHILE AT HIGH SCHOOL O.J. MAYO WAS CONSIDERED BY SEVERAL MEDIA OUTLETS TO BE THE BEST HIGH SCHOOL BASKETBALL PLAYER IN THE U.S. ___

10 STEPHEN CURRY LED THE NATION IN SCORING WHILE AT DAVIDSON COLLEGE (BASKETBALL). ___

RAIDER ROYALTY

PICTURED BELOW ARE SOME OF THE BLACK PLAYERS THAT COMPOSED THE CHAMPIONSHIP OAKLAND RAIDERS FOOTBALL TEAM (AUTHOR-CARTOONIST'S FAVORITE TEAM) OF THE 1960-70'S. OTHER PLAYERS APPEAR THROUGHOUT THE BOOK.

CLIFF BRANCH

WIDE RECEIVER OUT OF COLORADO UNIVERSITY BECAME NFL'S PREMIER WIDE RECEIVER DURING THE 1974 SEASON. HE WAS FIRST TEXAS HIGH SCHOOL SPRINTER TO RUN 9.3 FOR 100 YARDS.

JACK TATUM

RAIDERS NUMBER ONE PICK IN 1971, AT DEFENSIVE SAFETY OUT OF OHIO STATE. HE WAS HONORED ON ALL ROOKIE ALL PRO TEAM IN 1971, RUNNER UP AS ROOKIE OF THE YEAR.

Page Quiz

1) FINISH THE NAME QUIZ

ALVIN

□□□□ L □

NICKNAMED "THE DESTROYER" HE SPENT 11 YEARS AS ONE OF PRO BASKETBALL'S BEST DEFENSIVE GUARDS FOR THE GOLDEN STATE WARRIORS. HE COACHED THEM TO AN UPSET NBA CHAMPIONSHIP. HE RETIRED FROM COACHING AFTER 14 YEARS TO BECOME A VICE-PRESIDENT OF THE TEAM.

2) GUESS WHO QUIZ

THE FIRST WOMAN'S NAT'L. BASKETBALL LEAGUE PLAYER TO SUCCESSFULLY COMPLETE A SLAM DUNK WAS:

A.) YOLANDA GRIFFITH

B.) LISA LESLIE

C.) NICOLE POWELL

3) GUESS WHICH QUIZ

KIRBY PUCKETT

CARRIED HIS TEAM TO TWO WORLD SERIES BEFORE HIS CAREER WAS CUT SHORT BY GLAUCOMA. HE THEN DIED OF A STROKE AT 45.

HE PLAYED BUT FOR ONE TEAM THROUGH OUT HIS MAJOR LEAGUE CAREER.

A.) LOS ANGELES ANGELS

B.) MILWAUKEE

C.) MINNESOTA TWINS

CAL HALL OF FAMER

DR. EARL ROBINSON

IN 1957 HE PLAYED SHORTSTOP FOR THE UNIV. OF CAL. AT BERKELEY'S COLLEGE WORLD SERIES CHAMPIONSHIP TEAM. IN 1960 HE BECAME THE FIRST BLACK BASEBALL PLAYER TO EVER RECEIVE A SIGNING BONUS. (L.A. DODGERS).

HE WAS INDUCTED IN CAL HALL OF FAME

MEDIA

WENDELL SMITH

HE FOUGHT BASEBALL'S DISCRIMINATION WITH HIS PEN FOR OVER 35 YEARS (1937-1972). HE WAS THE FIRST AFRICAN-AMERICAN SPORTS WRITER TO BE INSTALLED INTO THE WRITERS WING OF THE BASEBALL HALL OF FAME IN COOPERSTOWN, N.Y.

Uncovered

John Wesley Donaldson
1891-1970

While playing profession Negro League baseball for the Kansas City Monarchs, Chicago American Giants, Tennessee Rats and others he was credited with 11 no hitters, a perfect game, and dozens of one hitters, he had two 20 strikeout games, 11 games with more that 25 strike outs, 30 games with more than 20 strikeouts, 109 games with more than 15 strikeouts.

He could also hit well, batting 334 in over 1,800 at bat.

Benjamin Boukpeti

Of Togo, a tiny West African Nation, took third place in Men's kayak winning the first ever medal for Togo at the Beijing Olympic Games

Cullen Jones

Won a Gold Medal in the 400 meter free style at the 2008 Beijing Olympic games, Helping to shatter the stereotype that blacks cant swim.

He's the third African-American swimmer to make the Olympic squad. Anthony Erin was the first in 2000.

Benny Barnes

A star athlete at Kennedy high school in Richmond (CA) and a two-sport (Football and Track) All-Conference player.

Entering in Stanford University where his team won two Rose Bowls.

Drafted by the Dallas Cowboys and appeared in three Super Bowls.

He was elected to the Community College Athletic Association Hall of Fame.

Final Notes

Anthony Mark Robles Born with only one leg, Arizona State University has become NCAA wrestling 125 pound champion. He was undefeated in the tournament he has over 100 wins in his career

TONI STONE

Toni Stone (Born Marcenia Lyle Alberga) was the first black woman to play pro ball when she signed with the Negro League to play second base.

The Philadelphia youth polo team The Cowtown/ work to ride based in Fairmount Park, an all black team...

...Won the 42nd Annual USPA National inter Scholastic Championship tournament in Charlottesville, VA

Burl Toler who starred with Ollie Matson on the undefeated university of San Francisco football team (1951) became the first black official in the national football league.

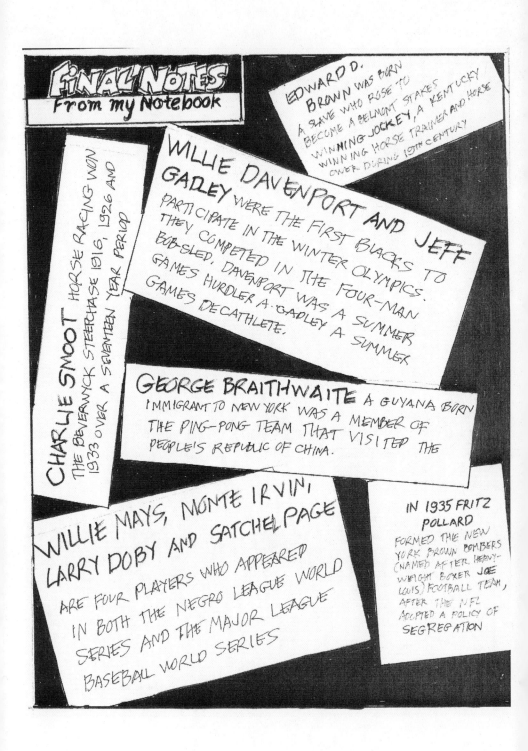

FINAL NOTES From my Notebook

EDWARD D. BROWN WAS BORN A SLAVE WHO ROSE TO BECOME A BELMONT STAKES WINNING JOCKEY, A KENTUCKY WINNING HORSE TRAINER AND HORSE OWER DURING 19TH CENTURY

WILLIE DAVENPORT AND JEFF GADLEY WERE THE FIRST BLACKS TO PARTICIPATE IN THE WINTER OLYMPICS. THEY COMPETED IN THE FOUR-MAN BOB-SLED, DAVENPORT WAS A SUMMER GAMES HURDLER A. GADLEY A SUMMER GAMES DECATHLETE.

CHARLIE SMOOT HORSE RACING WON THE BEVERWYCK STEEPLECHASE 1916, 1926 AND 1933 OVER A SEVENTEEN YEAR PERIOD

GEORGE BRAITHWAITE A GUYANA BORN IMMIGRANT TO NEW YORK WAS A MEMBER OF THE PING-PONG TEAM THAT VISITED THE PEOPLE'S REPUBLIC OF CHINA.

WILLIE MAYS, MONTE IRVIN, LARRY DOBY AND SATCHEL PAGE ARE FOUR PLAYERS WHO APPEARED IN BOTH THE NEGRO LEAGUE WORLD SERIES AND THE MAJOR LEAGUE BASEBALL WORLD SERIES

IN 1935 FRITZ POLLARD FORMED THE NEW YORK BROWN BOMBERS (NAMED AFTER HEAVY-WEIGHT BOXER JOE LOUIS) FOOTBALL TEAM, AFTER THE NFL ADOPTED A POLICY OF SEGREGATION

Answer Page I

Baseball Pages

<u>Page 1</u>
Scramble Quiz
1-Curt Flood
2-Joe Morgan

<u>Page 3</u>
Baseball Quiz
1-B   2-A
Who Am I? C-Josh Gibson

<u>Page 4</u>
Nickname Quiz
1-E   6-D
2-G   7-I
3-F   8-A
4-J   9-C
5-H   10-B

<u>Page 6</u>
Diamond Quiz
1-B   2-C   3-A

<u>Page 7</u>
Who Am I? B-Vida Blue

<u>Page 9</u>
Who Are They?
1-C   2-A   3-B
4-A   5-C

<u>Page 10</u>
Black Aces Quiz
1-B   2-F   3-H
4-J   5-I   6-A
7-B   8-D   9-C
10-D   11-E   12-D
13-G   14-F

<u>Page 16</u>
Stopper Quiz

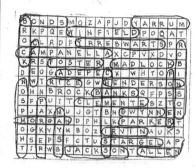

<u>Page 17</u>
Hardball Quiz
1-B   2-B

<u>Page 19</u>
Passport Quiz
1-A   2-B   3-C
4-B   5-B   6-B
7-B   8-B

<u>Page 20</u>
Negro League Quiz I
1-B   2-B
Who Am I?
C-Leroy "Satchel" Paige

<u>Page 21</u>
Negro League Quiz II
1-B   2-C   3-A

Answer Page II

Basketball Pages

Page 23
Basketball Quiz
1-A   2-B

Page 24
Basketball Scramble
1-Baylor
2-Robinson
3-Erving

Page 25
Round Ball Quiz
1-A   2-A

Page 26
Hardwood Quiz
1-B   2-A   3-A

Page 27-28
Basketball Scramble
1-Malone   2-Unseld
3-Frazier   4-Sampson
5-Gervin   6-Anthony
7-Curry   8-Howard
9-Mayo   10-Pierce
11-Evans

Page 29
Dunk Quiz
1-Reed   2-Miller
3-Iverson   4- Barkley
5-Duncan   6-Wilkes

Page 30
Basketball Nickname Quiz
1-D   2-E   3-F
4-H   5-G   6-A
7-C   8-B

Page 31
High School Match Quiz
1-A   2-E   3-H
4-B   5-C   6-J
7-I   8-D   9-F
10-G

Page 33
Which Globe Trotter Is He?
C-Marcus Haynes

Page 34
Legend Scramble Quiz
1-Gates   2-Lemon   3-Tatum

Page 35
Full Court Quiz
1-C   2-B   3-A
4-B   5-B

Boxing Pages

Page 38
Boxing Scramble Quiz
1-Tiger   2-Hearns

Page 40
Boxing Quiz
1-C   2-A   3-B

Page 41
Who Am I? C-Larry Holmes

Page 43
Prize Fighter Quiz
1-C   2-A   3-C
Who Am I? B-Ken Norton

Answer Page III

Football Pages

Page 45-46
Hall of Fame/Alumni Quiz

1-C	2-A	3-B
4-B	5-C	6-A
7-A	8-B	9-C

Page 47
Tailback Puzzle

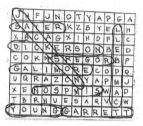

Page 48
QB Match Quiz

1-D	2-H	3-F
4-I	5-G	6-E
7-J	8-C	9-A
10-B		

Page 49
Heisman Trophy Quiz

1-E	2-J	3-E
4-F	5-I	6-G
7-K	8-E	9-D
10-H	11-H	12-E
13-C	14-B	

Page 50
Pigskin Parade
1-Washington
2-Upshaw
3-Strode

Page 52
Lineman Quiz

1-A	2-B
3-C	4-A

Page 53
Football Scramble Quiz
1-Sayers   2-Motley   3-Ford
Who Am I? B-Jerry Rice

Page 54
Who Are They?
1-C
2-A
3-C

Page 56
Tailback Quiz
(Puzzle not included)

Page 57
Name the Ball Carrier Quiz
1-Johnson   2-Holland
3-Allen   4-Daniels

Page 58
Running Back Quiz

1-C	2-A

Who Am I? B-Ernie Davis

Page 60
Brain Game
1-Slater   2-Robeson
3-Black   4-Page

Track & Field Pages

Page 62
Track & Field Scramble
1-Williams   2-Cambell   3-Drew

Page 63
Who Are They?
1-B-Gail Devers
2-C-Harrison Dillard

Page 65
Track & Field Quiz (Continued)
(See Quiz on Page 71 for #1-3)
4-C   5-B   6-C

Page 66
Who Am I? B-Mal Whitfield

Page 67
Olympic Games Quiz-z-z
1-C   2-A   3-C

Page 68
Sprinter Quiz
1-B   2-B   3-A
Who Am I? C-George Poage

Page 71
Track Quiz
1-A   2-B   3-A

Page 71
Event Match Quiz
1-D   2-H   3-G
4-A   5-B   6-C
7-E   8-F

Page 73
Black Stars Quiz
1-B   2-A   3-A

Nation Match Quiz
1-C   2-G   3-D
4-A   5-B   6-E
7-F

Page 76
Long Distance Runners
1-A   2-A   3-B
4-C   5-B   6-A

Page 78
Women in the Olympics Scramble
1-Rudolph   2-Jones   3-White

Other Sports

Page 80
Golf Scramble
1-Peete   2-Elder   3-Sifford

Page 83
Hockey Scramble Quiz
1-Fuhr   2-McKegney
3-Neufeld   4-White

Page 85
Tennis Quiz
1-C   2-C

Page 90
Who Am I? B- Shane Mosely

BILL RUSSELL, A GRADUATE OF McCLYMONDS HI SCHOOL, OAKLAND CA. HE BECAME UNSTOPPABLE FORCE IN NCAA BASKETBALL LEADING HIS TEAM TO TWO CHAMPIONSHIPS, AND 56 STRAIGHT VICTORIES.

3-20

HE WAS DRAFTED FIRST IN THE 1956 NBA DRAFT TO THE ST. LOUIS HAWKS, AND TRADED PRE-SEASON TO THE BOSTON CELTICS. HE CAPTAINED ...

THE U.S. OLYMPIC TEAM AND WON 11 WORLD CHAMPIONSHIPS IN 13 YEARS 8 CONSECUTIVE NBA CHAMPIONSHIPS.

SOUL CIRCLE

BILL RUSSELL

Answer Page V

Page 103
Potpourri
1-T   2-T   3-T
4-F) Played high school basketball
in Alameda, CA
5-T
6-F) known for his speed and base
stealing
7-T
8-T
9-F) Mets
10-F) Golden State Warriors

Page 104
Star Scramble
1-Thomas   2-Pele

Page 105
Athletes Puzzle

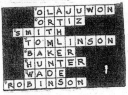

Page 106
Coaches Corner
1-F   2-J   3-I
4-G   5-H   6-C
7-B   8-A   9-E
10-D

Page 107
Sports Quiz
1-B   2-C   3-A
Who Am I? C-Major Taylor

Page 108
Name the Athlete Quiz
1-Woodard
2-Gibson
3-Swoopes

Page 109
Jersey Number Quiz
A-22   B-44   C-32
D-8   E-34   F-42
G-80   H-24   I-20
J-23

Page 110
Media Quiz
1-B   2-A   3-C
4-A   5-A

Page 111
True or False
1-T   2-T   3-T
4-T   5-F   6-T
7-T   8-T   9-T
10-T

Page 112
Last Page Quiz
1-Attles
2-B Lisa Leslie
3-C Minnesota Twins

- 121 -

INDEX

BASEBALL

Henry "Hank" Aaron, **3, 109**
Richie Allen, **9**
Felipe Alou, **106**
Emmett Ashford, **13**
Gene Baker, **105**
"Dusty" Baker, **106**
Dan Bankhead, **1, 12, 20**
Ernie Banks, **12**
James "Cool Papa" Bell, **4, 20**
Vida Blue, **7, 10**
Barry Bonds, **7**
Lou Brock, **6, 9**
Roy Campanella, **12**
Rod Carew, **95**
Orlando Cepeda, **6**
Jimmy Claxton, **108**
Roberto Clemente, **17**
Len Coleman, **12**
Ray Dandridge, **21**
Martin Dihigo, **21**
Larry Doby, **2, 116**
John Wesley Donaldson, **113**
Al Downing, **10**
Luke Easter, **92**
Cecil Fielder, **18**
Prince Fielder, **18, 111**
Curt Flood, **1**
Andrew "Robe" Foster, **4, 21**
George Foster, **95**
Cito Gaston, **106**
Bob Gibson, **2, 3, 10**
Dwight Gooden, **10, 102**
Jim "Mudcat" Grant, **10**
Pumpsie Green, **93**
Rickey Henderson, **6**
Ryan Howard, **18**
Elston Howard, **7**
Monte Irvin, **6, 116**
Reggie Jackson, **3, 4**
Ferguson Jenkins, **7, 10**
Derek Jeter, **18**
"Judy" Johnson, **21**

William Johnson, **4**
Sharon Richardson Jones, **4**
Sam Jones, **6, 10**
Derrek Lee, **18, 111**
Walter "Buck" Leonard, **4, 20**
John Henry Lloyd, **4**
Bill Madlock, **9**
Effa Manley, **100**
Juan Marichal, **10**
Pedro Martinez, **19**
Willie Mays, **4, 6, 12, 17, 109, 116**
Willie McCovey, **4, 13**
Joe Morgan, **1**
Don Newcombe, **6, 10, 20**
Mike Norris, **10**
Buck O'Neil, **102**
David Ortiz, **19, 105**
Leroy "Sachel" Paige, **4, 20, 116**
Dave Parker, **16**
Tony Perez, **106**
Vada Pinson, **2**
Kirby Puckett, **112**
Albert Pujols, **19**
Manny Ramirez, **19**
Edgar Renteria, **19**
Jim Rice, **95**
J.R. Richard, **10, 13**
Jackie Robinson, **1, 109**
"Dr." Earl Robinson, **112**
Frank Robinson, **4**
John Roosevelt Robinson, **4**
Jimmy Rollins, **18**
C. C. Sabathia, **18**
Pablo Sandoval, **19**
Ozzie Smith, **105**
Wendell Smith, **112**
Willie Stargell, **9**
Dave Stewart, **10**
Toni Stone, **88, 114**
Darryl Strawberry, **9**
Miguel Tejada, **19, 111**
Frank Thomas, **102, 103**
Hank Thompson, **6**
Juan Uribe, **19**
Moses Fleetwood Walker, **2**
Bill White, **3, 13**

Ken Williams, **12**
Dontrelle Willis, **10**
Maury Wills, **13, 102, 103**
Earl Wilson, **10**

BASKETBALL

Kareem Abdul-Jabbar, **25**
Ray Allen, **110**
Carmello Anthony, **28, 111**
Alvin Attles, **25, 112**
Charles Barkley, **29**
Don Barksdale, **24**
Don Barnette, **34**
Elgin Baylor, **24**
Manute Bol, **97**
Ruthie Bolton, **35**
Rebekkah Brunson, **35**
Kobe Bryant, **26, 31, 109**
Andrew Bynum, **31**
Wilt Chamberlain, **25, 30**
Nathaniel Clifton, **30**
Chuck Cooper, **30**
George Crowe, **97**
Stephen Curry, **28, 111**
Darryl Dawkins, **31**
Robert J. Douglas, **33, 115**
Tim Duncan, **29**
Monta Ellis, **31, 89**
Wayne Embry, **25**
Julius Erving, **24, 30**
Tyreke Evans, **28**
Walt Frazier, **27**
Clarence Gaines, **30**
Kevin Garnett, **31**
William "Pop" Gates, **34**
George Gervin, **27**
George Gregory, **30**
Blake Griffin, **97**
Yolanda Griffith, **36**
Bobby Hall, **30**
Marques Haynes, **33**
Chamique Holdsclaw, **35**
Dwight Howard, **28**
Billy Hunter, **105**
Allen Iverson, **29**

LeBron James, **31**
Avery Johnson, **106**
Earvin "Magic" Johnson, **23**
Kevin Johnson, **32**
K. C. Jones, **106**
Michael Jordan, **25, 109**
Jason Kidd, **102, 103**
William "Dolly" King, **92**
Kara Lawson, **36**
Meadowlark Lemon, **34**
Lisa Leslie, **36, 111**
Rashard Lewis, **31**
Earl Lloyd, **30**
Moses Malone, **27, 31**
O. J. Mayo, **28, 111**
Tracy McGrady, **31**
Johnny McLendon, **23**
Darius Miles, **31**
Reggie Miller, **29**
Earl Monroe, **26**
Dikembe Mutombo, **32**
Hakeem Olajuwon, **105**
Shaquille O'Neal, **26**
Jermaine O'Neal, **31**
Violet Palmer, **100**
Chris Paul, **110**
Paul Pierce, **28, 111**
Nicole Powell, **36**
Willis Reed, **29**
David Robinson, **96, 105**
Oscar Robinson, **24, 26**
Derrick Rose, **35**
Bill Russell, **23**
Ralph Sampson, **27**
Fred Snowden, **30**
Sheryl Swoopes, **108**
Reece "Goose" Tatum, **30, 34**
Isaiah Thomas, **23**
John Thompson, **24**
Nate Thurmond, **102**
Wes Unseld, **27**
Dwayne Wade, **105**
Demya Walker, **35**
John Wall, **96**
Chris Webber, **102, 103**
Lenny Wilkens, **106**

Dominique Wilkes, **29**
Lynette Woodard, **108**

BOXING

Dick Tiger, **38**
Muhammad Ali, **40, 43**
Kid Chocolate, **92**
George Dixon, **40**
Tiger Flowers, **40**
Joe Frazier, **41**
Joe Gans, **38**
Thomas Hearns, **38**
Larry Holmes, **41**
Evander Holyfield, **43**
Joe Jeannette, **41**
Roy Jones Jr., **89**
John Henry Lewis, **41**
Lennox Lewis, **110**
Sonny Liston, **43**
Joe Louis, **38**
Floyd Mayweather, **89**
Sam McVey, **92**
Shane Mosley, **90**
Floyd Patterson, **40, 43**
Bill Richmond, **92**
Sugar Ray Robinson, **40, 97**
Mike Tyson, **41, 43**
Andre Ward, **43**

FOOTBALL

Marcus Allen, **49, 57**
Benny Barnes, **113**
Lem Barney, **46**
Bobby Bell, **52**
Joe Black, **60**
Mel Blount, **46**
Cliff Branch, **111**
Marlin Briscoe, **48**
Willie Brown, **45, 95**
Roosevelt "Rosey" Brown, **45**
Tim Brown, **49**
Jim Brown, **55**
Buck Buchanan, **46**
Reggie Bush, **49**

Earl Campbell, **47, 49**
Annice Canady, **100**
Raymond Chester, **95**
Romeo Crennel, **106**
Daunte Culpepper, **48**
Clem Daniels, **57**
Ernie Davis, **49, 58**
Ron Dayne, **49**
Eric Dickerson, **47**
Tony Dorsett, **49, 56**
Tony Dungy, **106**
Vince Evans, **48**
Charles W. Follis, **45**
Len Ford, **53**
Willie Galimore, **55**
Mike Garrett, **49, 55, 102, 103**
Joe Gilliam, **48**
James Harris, **48**
Jerome "Brud" Holland, **57**
Ken Houston, **46**
Bo Jackson, **47**
Hue Jackson, **90**
Willie Jeffries, **54**
John Henry Johnson, **57**
Deacon Jones, **45**
Dick Lane, **54**
Willie Lanier, **46**
Larry Little, **46**
Ollie Matson, **54, 114**
Harry McDonald, **92**
Donovan McNabb, **48**
Steve McNair, **48**
Marion Motley, **53**
Warren Moon, **48**
Ozzie Newsome, **102**
Cam Newton, **93**
Alan Page, **60**
Jim Parker, **52**
Walter Payton, **56, 58, 109**
Joe Perry, **56**
Natalie Randolph, **93**
Jerry Rice, **53, 109**
Paul Robeson, **60**
Johnny Rogers, **49, 58**
George Rogers, **49**
Mike Rozier, **49**

Barry Sanders, **109**
Gale Sayers, **53, 55**
David Shaw, **89**
Art Shell, **106**
O. J. Simpson, **47, 49**
Billy Sims, **49**
Mike Singletary, **93**
Fred "Duke" Slater, **60**
Emmitt Smith, **56, 109**
Louie Smith, **98, 106**
Woody Strode, **50**
Jack Tatum, **111**
Lawrence Taylor, **52**
Burl Toler, **114**
Mike Tomlin, **98**
LaDainian Tomlinson, **105**
Johnny Unitas, **52**
Eugene Upshaw, **50**
Michael Vick, **48, 93**
Herschel Walker, **49**
Kenny Washington, **50**
Doug Williams, **48, 54**
Tyrone Willingham, **106**
Bill Willis, **52**
Vince Young, **98**
Claude "Buddy" Young, **55**

TRACK & FIELD

Donovan Bailey, **73**
Bernard Barmasai, **76**
Benny Barnes, **113**
Bob Beamon, **64, 67**
Kenenisa Bekele, **110**
Abebe Bikila, **65, 73, 75**
Usain Bolt, **69**
John Borican, **92**
Ralph Boston, **67**
Lee Calhoun, **66, 67, 70**
Milton Campbell, **62, 67, 71**
Linford Christie, **73**
Alice Coachman, **71**
Willie Davenport, **65, 71**
Meseret Defar, **76**
Anita L. DeFrantz, **100**
Dr. Evie Dennis, **89**

Gail Devers, **63**
Harrison Dillard, **63**
Howard Drew, **62**
Charles Dumas, **71**
Lee Evans, **68**
Barney Ewell, **95**
Mohammed Farah, **76**
Allyson Felix, **69**
Shelly Ann Frasier, **90**
Jeff Gadley, **65**
Justin Gatlin, **90**
Tyson Gay, **90**
Haile Gebrselassie, **76**
Maurice Greene, **70**
Florence Griffith Joyner, **77**
Bob Hayes, **70, 71**
Stephanie Hightower, **89**
Jim Hines, **95**
Chaunte Howard, **69**
DeHart Hubbard, **64, 71**
Martha Hudson, **77**
Franklin Jacobs, **64**
Regina Jacobs, **77**
Charlie Jenkins, **71**
Rafer Johnson, **65, 67**
Ben Johnson, **71, 73**
Michael Johnson, **68**
Barbara Jones, **77**
Marion Jones, **78**
Jackie Joyner Kersee, **78**
Alberto Juantorena, **73**
Kipchoge Keino, **76**
Mary Jepkosgei Keitany, **74**
Duncan Kibet, **75**
Moses Kiptanui, **76**
James Kwambai, **74**
Lloyd LaBeach, **73**
Bernard Legat, **69**
Joe Lashley, **107**
Carl Lewis, **63**
Steve Lewis, **64**
Ralph Metcalfe, **60, 65, 67**
LaShawn Merritt, **97, 111**
Jearl Miles Clark, **69**
Catherine Ndereba, **75**
Jesse Owens, **62, 67, 72**

Eulace Peacock, **70**
Marie-José Pérec, **73**
Dwight Phillips, **96**
George Poage, **68**
Asafa Powell, **110**
Mike Powell, **70**
George Rhoden, **73**
Sanya Richards, **89**
Fatuma Roba, **73, 74**
Wilma Rudolph, **77, 78**
Evans Rutto, **74**
Javier Sotomayor, **64**
Andy Stanfield, **70, 71**
Willie Steele, **71**
John Baxter "Doc" Taylor Jr., **68**
Paul Kibii Tergat, **74**
Eddie Tolan, **66**
Derartu Tulu, **75**
Wyomia Tyus, **77**
Dr. LeRoy Walker, **72**
Willie White, **78**
Mal Whitfield, **66**
Archie Williams, **62**
Lucinda Williams, **77**
John Woodruff, **68, 71**

WOMEN

Ruthie Bolton, **35**
Rebekkah Brunson, **35**
Annice Canady, **100**
Alice Coachman, **71**
Juliet Cuthbert, **63**
Cheryl Daniels, **107**
Dominique Dawes, **98**
Meseret Defar, **76**
Anita L. DeFrantz, **100**
Dr. Evie Dennis, **89**
Gail Devers, **63**
Diane Durham, **107**
Nikki Franke, **88**
Allyson Felix, **69**
Shelly Ann Frasier, **90**
Zina Garrison, **86**
Althea Gibson, **85, 108**
Yolanda Griffith, **36**

Florence Griffith Joyner, **83**
Stephanie Hightower, **89**
Chamique Holdsclaw, **35**
Chaunte Howard, **69**
Martha Hudson, **77**
Flo Hyman, **104**
Regina Jacobs, **77**
Barbara Jones, **77**
Marion Jones, **78**
Jackie Joyner Kersee, **78**
Mary Jepkosgei Keitany, **74**
Kara Lawson, **36**
Lisa Leslie, **36, 111**
Effa Manley, **100**
Jearl Miles Clark, **69**
Catherine Ndereba, **75**
Iris Smith, **100**
Violet Palmer, **100**
Marie-José Pérec, **73**
Nicole Powell, **36**
Natalie Randolph, **93**
Sanya Richards, **89**
Fatuma Roba, **73, 74**
Wilma Rudolph, **77, 78**
Iris Smith, **100**
Toni Stone, **88, 114**
Sheryl Swoopes, **108**
Debbie Thomas, **104**
Derartu Tulu, **75**
Wyomia Tyus, **77**
Demya Walker, **35**
Ora Washington, **85, 86**
Willie White, **78**
Lucinda Williams, **77**
Serena Williams, **85**
Venus Williams, **85, 111**
Lynette Woodard, **108**

OTHER SPORTS

BILLIARDS
  Cisero Murphy, **88**

BOWLING
  Cheryl Daniels, **107**
  George Branham III, **104**

LIVING LEGEND AWARD

Mr. Morrie Turner

Morrie Turner spends his life doing good and doing it well. Whether serving his country in WWII, assisting the police force, entertainning troops overseas, or gently lecturing children on the value of their education, Morrie does it all with radiant energy and warm humor. His knack for making a point concisely and memorably, as demonstrated in his countless contributions to humanitarian causes, has earned him numerous honors. Among them are the California Public Education Hall of Fame, Delta Society of Journalism Award, Police Activities League Award, National Conference of Christians and Jews Award, Black Filmmakers Hall of Fame, Oakland Symphony Young People's Concert Award, and the Brotherhood Award from the National Cartoonist Society.

Perhaps his biggest contribution, however, is his creation of Wee Pals, the world's first syndicated comic strip to feature a multi-ethnic cast of characters. Using humor from his own African American experience, Morrie first free-lanced cartoons to Black newspapers and magazines such as Ebony and the Chicago Defender. Finally, inspired by cartoonist Charles Schulz and encouraged by comedian Dick Gregory, Morrie launched Wee Pals in 1965. The strip quickly starred in hundreds of newspapers, dozens of books, greeting cards, toys and the weekly animated television cartoon series, Kid Power. The cast of Wee Pals represents many different races and abilities, even the token young bigot takes the stage occasionally. Morrie coined the term "Rainbow Power," under the banner of which all of his young players march.

With nimble word play, a deceptively simple drawing style, and a clear perception and love of humanity, Morrie shows us a world where people can live, learn, work and play together, regardless of racial, religious, sexual or physical differences. It is a world he embraces genuinely, deeply, and invites his audience to gladly do the same.

The Oakland Alliance of Black Educators salutes the creative genius of Morrie Turner as he continues to educate our village.

ABOUT THE AUTHOR

Morrie Turner was born on December 11, 1923, in Oakland, California, the youngest of four sons to James "George" and Nora Turner. He lived in West Oakland during the Great Depression.

He served in the U.S. Air Force during World War II. At one point, he tested to become a pilot in the Tuskegee Airmen program but washed out during the final test. He subsequently joined the all-Black 477th Bomber group and became the group's newspaper cartoonist.

After the war ended, Morrie returned to Oakland and married his lifetime sweetheart, Letha, who gave birth to their son, Morris. He worked as a police clerk in the Oakland Police Department and continued to do freelance cartoons for magazines and trade publications, including *Black World* and *Ebony*.

Several years later, his meeting with Charles Shultz, creator of the popular "Peanuts" cartoon, had a major influence in Morrie's creation of an all-Black comic strip, "Dinky Fellas," which was sold to the *Chicago Defender*. The Lew Little Syndicate discovered the strip on February 15, 1965, and contracted it as the nation's first truly integrated strip.

When Martin Luther King, Jr. was assassinated in April 1968, Morrie's comic strip "Wee Pals" was in only five major newspapers. Three months after King's death, the strip appeared in more than 100 newspapers.

The success of "Wee Pals" led to dozens of books and an animated television series, "Kid Power." It was during this period that Morrie created the phrase "rainbow power," which meant the power of all colors working together.

Morrie is the recipient of the Anti-Defamation League's Humanitarian Award, the Boys and Girls Club Image Award, the B'nai Brith Humanitarian Award, the California Educator's Award, the Sparky Award, given by the Cartoon Art Museum, and the Milton Caniff Lifetime Achievement Award, presented by the National Cartoonist Society. He is also the subject of a documentary titled *Keep the Faith with Morrie*.

In 1970, Morrie served as vice-chair of the media forum for the White House Conference on Children. Fred Rogers (of "Mr. Rogers' Neighborhood") was chair.